PERFECT COOKING WITH LAMB & PORK

GOOD HOUSEKEEPING
STEP-BY-STEP COOKERY

PERFECT COOKING WITH LAMB & PORK

Guild Publishing/Ebury Press
LONDON

This edition published 1986 by
Book Club Associates
By arrangement with Ebury Press

Consultant editor: Jeni Wright
Editors: Veronica Sperling and Barbara Croxford
Design: Mike Leaman
Illustrations: John Woodcock and Kate Simunek
Photography: David Johnson
Cookery: Susanna Tee, Maxine Clark, Janet Smith

Cover photograph: Roast Knuckle of Pork (page 131)

Filmset by Advanced Filmsetters (Glasgow) Ltd

Printed and bound in Italy by
New Interlitho, S.p.a., Milan

CONTENTS

INTRODUCTION	7
ROASTS AND POT ROASTS	8
ALL WRAPPED UP	22
COLD PORK DISHES	36
QUICK AND LIGHT MEALS	50
CLASSIC DISHES	62
EVERYDAY DISHES	88
ENTERTAINING	114

USEFUL INFORMATION AND BASIC RECIPES

GUIDE TO CUTS, COOKING METHODS AND TECHNIQUES	130
CARVING	138
GUIDE TO BACON, GAMMON AND HAM	140
FREEZING	142
SAUCES AND FLAVOURINGS	144
PÂTÉS, TERRINES AND SAUSAGES	150
VEGETABLE AND FRUIT DISHES	152
BASIC RECIPES	156
INDEX	159

COOKERY NOTES

Follow *either* metric *or* imperial *measures for the recipes in this book as they are not inter-changeable.* Sets of spoon measures are available in both metric and imperial size to give accurate measurement of small quantities. All spoon measures are level unless otherwise stated. When measuring milk we have used the exact conversion of 568 ml (1 pint).

* Size 4 eggs should be used except when otherwise stated.

† Granulated sugar is used un-less otherwise stated.

● Plain flour is used unless otherwise stated.

OVEN TEMPERATURE CHART

°C	°F	Gas mark
110	225	$\frac{1}{4}$
130	250	$\frac{1}{2}$
140	275	1
150	300	2
170	325	3
180	350	4
190	375	5
200	400	6
220	425	7
230	450	8
240	475	9

KEY TO SYMBOLS

$\boxed{1.00*}$ Indicates minimum preparation and cooking times in hours and minutes. They do not include prepared items in the list of ingredients; calcu-lated times apply only to the method. An asterisk * indicates extra time should be allowed, so check the note below symbols.

⌂ Chef's hats indicate degree of difficulty of a recipe: no hat means it is straightforward; one hat slightly more complicated; two hats indicates that it is for more advanced cooks.

£ Indicates a recipe which is good value for money; £ £ indicates an expensive recipe. No £ sign indicates an inexpensive recipe.

✱ Indicates that a recipe will freeze. If there is no symbol, the recipe is unsuitable for freezing. An asterisk * indicates special freezer instructions so check the note immediately below the symbols.

$\boxed{\text{309 cals}}$ Indicates calories per serving, including any sugges-tions (e.g. cream, to serve) given in the ingredients.

METRIC CONVERSION SCALE

LIQUID			SOLID		
Imperial	Exact conversion	Recommended ml	Imperial	Exact conversion	Recommended g
$\frac{1}{4}$ pint	142 ml	150 ml	1 oz	28.35 g	25 g
$\frac{1}{2}$ pint	284 ml	300 ml	2 oz	56.7 g	50 g
1 pint	568 ml	600 ml	4 oz	113.4 g	100 g
$1\frac{1}{2}$ pints	851 ml	900 ml	8 oz	226.8 g	225 g
$1\frac{3}{4}$ pints	992 ml	1 litre	12 oz	340.2 g	350 g
For quantities of $1\frac{3}{4}$ pints and over,			14 oz	397.0 g	400 g
litres and fractions of a litre have			16 oz (1 lb)	453.6 g	450 g
been used.			1 kilogram (kg) equals 2.2 lb.		

PERFECT COOKING WITH LAMB AND PORK

In this volume you will find some of the best lamb and pork recipes ever written, from everyday family meals to deliciously different dinner party dishes. Lamb and pork are such versatile meats: choose from simple Roasts and Pot Roasts, unusual ideas in All Wrapped Up, tasty Cold Pork Dishes, useful Quick and Light Meals, time-honoured Classics and exotic ideas for Entertaining. Each recipe is photographed in colour, and there are step-by-step illustrations to guide you smoothly through the methods, plus menu suggestions to help with serving and accompaniments.

The tinted section at the back of the book is packed with information on cooking perfect lamb and pork. Cuts, Cooking Methods and Techniques are covered in detail, plus step-by-steps on Carving, how to make Pâtés, Terrines and Sausages, and useful advice on Freezing lamb and pork. There's an informative guide to Bacon, Gammon and Ham, plus recipes for Sauces and Flavourings, Vegetable and Fruit Dishes to serve as accompaniments, and an immensely useful section of Basic Recipes.

Roasts and Pot Roasts

Roasts and pot roasts make for carefree cooking. Once the meat is in the oven, you can go away and forget about it. Just the thing for days when you are busy and the cooking needs to look after itself. And with pot roasts, even the less prime cuts of lamb and pork will be mouth-wateringly tender.

CROWN ROAST OF LAMB

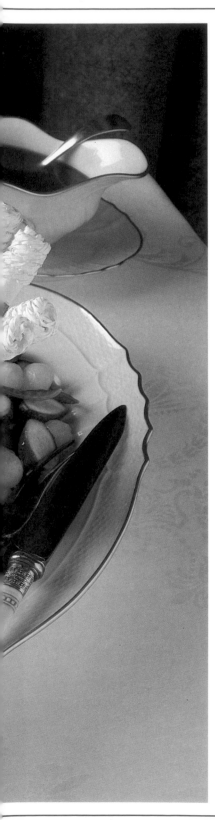

| 2.15 | 🍴 🍴 | £ £ | 427–640 cals |

Serves 4–6

2 best end necks of lamb,
    chined, each with 6–8 cutlets

75 g (3 oz) long grain rice

salt and freshly ground pepper

25 g (1 oz) butter or margarine

1 small onion, skinned and finely
    chopped

3 celery sticks, trimmed and finely
    chopped

1 eating apple, peeled, cored and
    finely chopped

1 small garlic clove, skinned and
    crushed

10 ml (2 tsp) curry powder

225 g (8 oz) fresh breadcrumbs,
    toasted

30 ml (2 tbsp) chopped fresh
    parsley

1 egg

50 g (2 oz) lard

30 ml (2 tbsp) plain flour

450 ml (¾ pint) beef stock

1 With a sharp, pointed knife, trim each cutlet bone to a depth of 2.5 cm (1 inch).

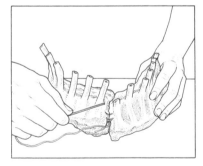

2 Bend the joints around, fat side inwards, and sew together using strong cotton or fine string to form a crown. Cover the exposed bones with foil.

3 Put the rice in a large saucepan of boiling salted water and cook for 12–15 minutes or until tender. Drain, then rinse well under cold running water.

4 Melt the butter in a saucepan, add the onion, celery, apple, garlic and curry powder and cook gently until the vegetables are softened.

5 Remove from the heat and stir in the breadcrumbs, parsley, cooked rice, egg and salt and pepper to taste. Allow to cool, then spoon into the centre of the crown roast. Weigh the joint and calculate the cooking time, allowing 25 minutes per 450 g (1 lb) plus an extra 25 minutes.

6 Melt the lard in a roasting tin then stand the lamb joint in the tin. Roast in the oven at 180°C (350°F) mark 4 for the calculated cooking time, basting occasionally. Cover the joint lightly with foil if the stuffing becomes too brown during roasting.

7 Transfer the crown roast to a warmed serving dish and keep hot. Pour off all but 30 ml (2 tbsp) of the fat from the roasting tin, place the tin on top of the cooker and sprinkle in the flour. Blend well with a wooden spoon, then cook for 2–3 minutes, stirring continuously until golden brown. Gradually stir in the stock and bring to the boil. Simmer for 2–3 minutes, then add salt and pepper to taste. Pour into a gravy boat or jug and serve hot with the joint.

Menu Suggestion

Serve Crown Roast of Lamb for a special occasion meal. With its mildly curried stuffing, it goes well with a medley of courgettes and button onions, or an exotic vegetable such as aubergines or peppers stuffed with a mixture of spiced rice, nuts and raisins.

FRENCH ROAST RACKS OF LAMB WITH ROSEMARY AND GARLIC

| 2.00 | 🍴 | £ £ | 263–395 cals |

Serves 4–6

2 best end necks of lamb, chined, each with 6–8 cutlets

2 garlic cloves, skinned

60 ml (4 tbsp) whole grain mustard

30 ml (2 tbsp) olive or vegetable oil

30 ml (2 tbsp) chopped fresh rosemary or 15 ml (1 tbsp) dried

salt and freshly ground pepper

60–90 ml (4–6 tbsp) dried white breadcrumbs

1 With a sharp, pointed knife, trim the fat off the ends of the cutlets to expose about 5 cm (2 inches) of bone.

2 Cut the garlic cloves into slivers. Using a sharp, pointed knife, make small incisions into the surface of the lamb and insert a sliver of garlic in each. Place the racks, fat side up, in an oiled roasting tin.

3 Mix the mustard, oil, rosemary and salt and pepper to taste together in a small bowl. Spread this mixture over the lamb fat to cover it evenly.

4 Roast in the oven at 180°C (350°F) mark 4 for 1–1¼ hours, depending on the number of cutlets and according to how well done you like your lamb.

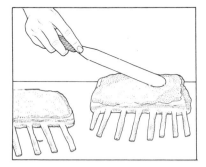

5 Remove the tin from the oven and sprinkle the breadcrumbs evenly over the mustard coating. Press firmly with a palette knife so that the crumbs adhere. Return the tin to the oven, increase the oven temperature to 200°C (400°F) mark 6 and roast for a further 15 minutes until crisp and golden brown.

6 Transfer the racks to a carving dish or board, leave to stand for 10–15 minutes at room temperature, then carve into individual cutlets.

Menu Suggestion

Simplicity is the keynote to this roast lamb dish. Serve for Sunday lunch, with French-style vegetables such as carrots and green beans tossed in chopped fresh herbs, and steamed new potatoes with melted butter.

MUSTARD-COATED LEG OF LAMB

2.15* £ £ 687 cals

* plus 6–8 hours marinating

Serves 6

75 ml (5 tbsp) Dijon mustard

5 ml (1 tsp) dried rosemary

2 garlic cloves, skinned and crushed

15 ml (1 tbsp) soy sauce

salt and freshly ground pepper

15 ml (1 tbsp) olive or vegetable oil

1.8 kg (4 lb) leg of lamb

300 ml (½ pint) lamb or beef stock

1 Put the mustard, rosemary, garlic, soy sauce, salt and pepper in a bowl and mix well together.

2 Gradually whisk in the oil, drop by drop, to make a thick cream consistency.

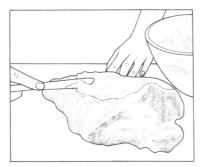

3 Spread the mustard mixture all over the lamb and put in a large shallow dish. Cover and marinate in the refrigerator for 6–8 hours.

4 Put the lamb, fat side up, on a rack in a roasting tin. Roast in the oven at 180°C (350°F) mark 4 for about 1¾ hours, or until the juices run clear when the thickest part of the meat is pierced with a skewer. Transfer the lamb to a warmed serving dish and keep hot.

5 Pour the stock into the roasting tin and stir to loosen the sediment. Bring to the boil, then simmer, stirring, until the sauce reduces slightly. Serve the lamb carved into slices, with the sauce handed separately.

Menu Suggestion

With its spicy coating of mustard and soy sauce, this roast leg of lamb makes an unusual alternative to an ordinary Sunday joint. Serve with roast potatoes cooked in the oven at the same time, and lightly cooked courgettes or mange-touts.

MUSTARD-COATED LEG OF LAMB

Dijon mustard is not essential for this recipe, but it does give the lamb a very special flavour. Dijon mustard is quite unique, being less strong than other types of mustard, especially the fiery hot, bright yellow varieties of English mustard. Dijon mustard was first made in the town of Dijon in Burgundy as long ago as the Middle Ages. It is made from dehusked black mustard seeds mixed with white wine (Burgundy is one of the most prolific wine producing areas of France), herbs and spices. The French are so proud of their Dijon mustard that it is controlled by an *appellation* in the same way as wine.

ROLLED STUFFED BREASTS OF LAMB

| 1.55 | £ ✳* | 925 cals |

* freeze at end of step 4

Serves 4

25 g (1 oz) butter or margarine

1 medium onion, skinned and
  chopped

25 g (1 oz) streaky bacon, rinded
  and chopped

226 g (8 oz) packet frozen leaf
  spinach, thawed

75 g (3 oz) fresh breadcrumbs

45 ml (3 tbsp) chopped fresh
  parsley

finely grated rind of $\frac{1}{2}$ lemon

15 ml (1 tbsp) lemon juice

pinch of grated nutmeg

1 egg, beaten

salt and freshly ground pepper

2 large breasts of lamb, boned and
  trimmed, total weight about
  1.1 kg (2$\frac{1}{2}$ lb)

45 ml (3 tbsp) vegetable oil

watercress, to garnish

1 Melt the butter in a saucepan,
add the onion and bacon and
fry for about 5 minutes until
lightly browned.

2 Drain the spinach and chop
roughly. Place in a bowl with
the onion and bacon, breadcrumbs, parsley, lemon rind and
juice, nutmeg and egg. Mix
together well, adding salt and
pepper to taste.

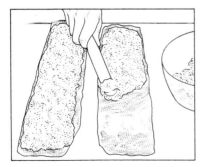

3 Lay the breasts of lamb fat
side down on a work surface
and spread the stuffing evenly
over them with a palette knife.

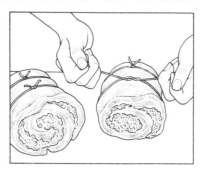

4 Roll up the lamb breasts
loosely and tie in several places
with string to hold their shape.

5 Weigh each joint and calculate
the cooking time, allowing 25
minutes per 450 g (1 lb) plus 25
minutes for each joint. Heat the oil
in a roasting tin and place the
joints in the tin. Roast in the oven
at 180°C (350°F) mark 4 for the
calculated cooking time, basting
occasionally. Serve hot, garnished
with watercress.

Menu Suggestion

Breast of lamb makes an
economical midweek roast. This
recipe has a spinach stuffing,
therefore only one or two
additional vegetables is necessary.
New potatoes tossed in mint
butter would go well, with glazed
carrots.

**ROLLED STUFFED
BREASTS OF LAMB**

Breast of lamb is one of the
fattier cuts, but it is excellent
cooked in this way with a tasty
and substantial stuffing. When
buying breasts of lamb, look for
the leanest ones possible—not all
lamb breasts are very fatty. Any
visible fat should be white and
dry, whereas the meat should be
pink and moist. Most lambs are
aged between 3 and 6 months at
the time of slaughtering, after
this time the meat darkens in
colour and becomes more
coarsely grained.

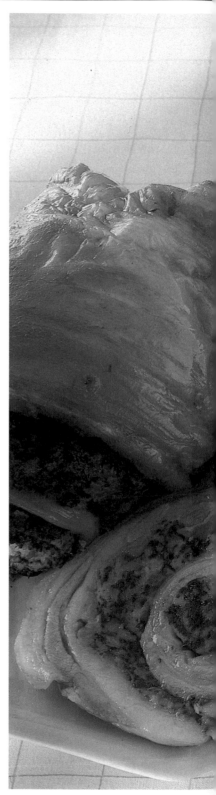

KIDNEY-STUFFED PORK LOIN

5.00* ☐ £ £ 523 cals

* plus overnight marinating and 15 minutes cooling

Serves 8

2.3 kg (5 lb) pork loin, boned with rind on
30 ml (2 tbsp) vegetable oil
300 ml ($\frac{1}{2}$ pint) dry white wine
2.5 ml ($\frac{1}{2}$ tsp) dried sage
2 bay leaves
1 garlic clove, skinned and crushed
8 juniper berries
salt and freshly ground pepper
2 lamb's kidneys
25 g (1 oz) butter or margarine
1 medium onion, skinned and finely chopped
100 g (4 oz) cooking apple, peeled, cored and finely chopped
100 g (4 oz) fresh breadcrumbs
finely grated rind of 1 lemon
30 ml (2 tbsp) lemon juice
1 egg, beaten
10 ml (2 tsp) plain flour

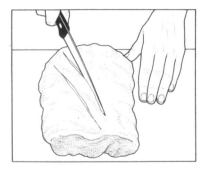

1 Remove the rind from the pork and reserve. Score the fat evenly. Lay the meat flat, fat side down, on a board or work surface.

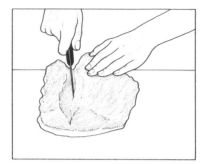

2 Slice lengthways, two-thirds through the thick side of the 'eye' of the meat. Open the joint up like a book.

3 Cut the reserved rind in strips. Place the meat in a non-stick shallow dish. Mix the oil, wine, sage, bay leaves, garlic, juniper berries and salt and pepper together in a jug and pour over the meat. Turn once, cover and marinate in the refrigerator overnight.

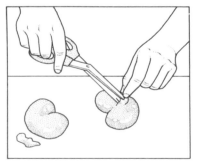

4 Using scissors, remove the core from the kidneys, then chop the flesh.

5 Melt the butter in a pan, add the onion and fry gently for about 5 minutes until browned. Add the kidney and apple and fry until the apple is soft. Stir in the breadcrumbs, lemon rind and juice, the egg and salt and pepper to taste. Leave to cool for 15 minutes.

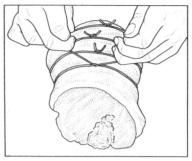

6 Remove the pork from the marinade and spread with the kidney stuffing. Form the joint into a roll and tie at close intervals. Reserve the marinade.

7 Weigh the joint and calculate the cooking time, allowing 35 minutes per 450 g (1 lb) plus 35 minutes. Place in an oiled roasting tin. Roast in the oven at 190°C (375°F) mark 5 for the calculated cooking time. Sprinkle the rind well with salt and cook for 1 hour above the roast.

8 Transfer the meat and crackling to a warmed serving dish and keep hot. Pour off all but 15 ml (1 tbsp) of the fat from the roasting tin, place the tin on top of the cooker and sprinkle in the flour. Blend well with a wooden spoon, then cook, for 2–3 minutes, stirring continuously until golden.

9 Strain the reserved marinade and gradually stir into the tin. Bring to the boil and simmer for 2–3 minutes, stirring, until the sediment is loosened and the gravy thickened. Serve the pork hot, with the gravy handed separately in a gravy boat or jug.

Menu Suggestion
Boned loin of pork is perfect for a dinner party main course, because it is so easy to carve. Serve with a layered potato dish, such as *gratin dauphinois*, and Ratatouille (page 152).

PEANUT GLAZED BACON HOCK

2.45	518 cals

Serves 6

1.1 kg (2½ lb) bacon hock
1 medium carrot, peeled and sliced
1 medium onion, skinned and quartered
1 bay leaf
30 ml (2 tbsp) lemon marmalade
30 ml (2 tbsp) demerara sugar
10 ml (2 tsp) lemon juice
dash of Worcestershire sauce
25 g (1 oz) salted peanuts, chopped

1 Put the bacon in a casserole with the carrot, onion and bay leaf. Pour in enough water to come half-way up the joint. Cover and cook in the oven at 180°C (350°F) mark 4 for about 2¼ hours.

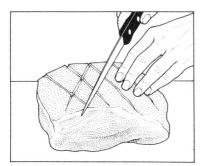

2 Remove the bacon from the casserole, carefully cut off and discard the rind, then score the fat with a sharp knife.

3 Put the marmalade, sugar, lemon juice and Worcestershire sauce in a bowl and mix well together with a wooden spoon.

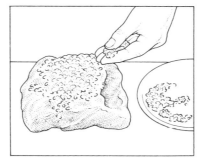

4 Spread the mixture over the surface of the joint. Sprinkle on the chopped peanuts.

5 Place the joint in a roasting tin. Increase the oven temperature to 220°C (425°F) mark 7 and return the joint to the oven for 15 minutes to glaze. Serve sliced.

Menu Suggestion
Glazed bacon is good for a family meal, served hot with seasonal vegetables. Alternatively, serve it sliced cold for a buffet party, with a selection of salads.

POT ROAST OF PORK AND RED CABBAGE

| 2.15 | 531 cals |

Serves 4

45 ml (3 tbsp) red wine vinegar

450 g (1 lb) red cabbage

225 g (8 oz) cooking apple

15 ml (1 tbsp) demerara sugar

15 ml (1 tbsp) plain flour

salt and freshly ground pepper

700 g (1½ lb) boneless pork shoulder, rinded

coriander sprigs, to garnish

1 Bring a large saucepan of water to the boil, to which 15 ml (1 tbsp) of the vinegar has been added.

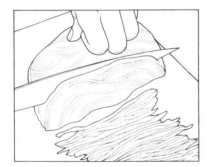

2 Meanwhile, shred the red cabbage. When the water is boiling, add the cabbage, bring back to the boil, then drain well.

3 Peel, core and slice the apple and place with the cabbage in a casserole just wide enough to take the pork joint.

4 Add the sugar, the remaining vinegar, the flour and salt and pepper to taste. Stir well together.

5 Slash the fat side of the joint several times and sprinkle with plenty of salt and pepper. Place on top of the cabbage and cover the casserole.

6 Cook in the oven at 190°C (375°F) mark 5 for about 1¾ hours, or until pork is tender. Serve the pork sliced on a warmed serving platter, surrounded by cabbage. Garnish with coriander and serve the remaining cabbage in a serving dish.

Menu Suggestion
This tasty dish is good served for an everyday evening meal, with a plain accompaniment such as creamed potatoes.

BACON IN CIDER WITH SAGE AND ONION DUMPLINGS

2.30	£	858 cals

Serves 6

1.1 kg (2½ lb) smoked collar of bacon
4 cloves
300 ml (½ pint) dry cider
1 bay leaf
125 g (4 oz) fresh white breadcrumbs
175 g (6 oz) self raising flour
50 g (2 oz) shredded suet
5 ml (1 tsp) rubbed sage
25 g (1 oz) butter or margarine
2 medium onions, skinned
salt and freshly ground pepper
parsley sprigs, to garnish

1 Place the bacon in a saucepan and cover with cold water. Bring slowly to the boil. Drain off the water. Pat the bacon dry.

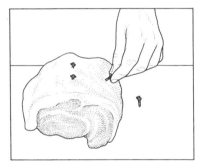

2 Slice off the rind if it is not cooked enough to peel away. Stud the fat with cloves.

3 Put the bacon in a shallow casserole with the cider and bay leaf. Cover tightly and cook in the oven at 180°C (350°F) mark 4 for 2¼ hours.

4 Meanwhile, mix the breadcrumbs, flour, suet and sage together in a bowl. Rub in the butter with your fingertips.

5 Coarsely grate in the onions. Bind to a soft dough with water, then add a little salt and freshly ground pepper.

6 Shape the dough into 12 dumplings. Forty-five minutes before the end of the cooking time, add the dumplings to the juices surrounding the bacon. Cover again and finish cooking. Serve the bacon sliced, with a little of the cooking liquid spooned over, surrounded by the dumplings. Garnish with parsley sprigs.

Menu Suggestion
With its sage and onion dumplings, this bacon dish is very substantial—ideal for a winter family supper. Serve with a seasonal green vegetable such as Brussels sprouts or spinach.

BAKED STUFFED LAMB'S HEARTS

3.20–3.50	£	425 cals

Serves 4

4 small lamb's hearts, total weight
    about 550 g (1¼ lb)

2 large onions, skinned

60 ml (4 tbsp) vegetable oil

50 g (2 oz) streaky bacon, rinded
    and chopped

50 g (2 oz) button mushrooms,
    chopped

50 g (2 oz) fresh breadcrumbs

finely grated rind of ½ lemon

15 ml (1 tbsp) lemon juice

30 ml (2 tbsp) chopped fresh
    parsley

salt and freshly ground pepper

2 carrots, peeled and sliced

300 ml (½ pint) lamb or chicken
    stock

15 ml (1 tbsp) tomato purée

chopped parsley and blanched
    julienne of lemon zest, to garnish

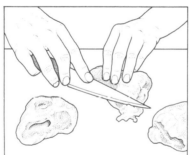

1 Wash the hearts thoroughly
under cold running water.
Trim them and remove any ducts.

2 Cut 1 of the onions in half
and chop 1 half finely. Heat
half of the oil in a frying pan, add
the chopped onion, bacon and
mushrooms and fry for about
5 minutes until the onion is
softened. Turn into a bowl, add
the breadcrumbs, lemon rind and
juice, parsley and salt and pepper
to taste. Mix well together. Leave
to cool for 10 minutes.

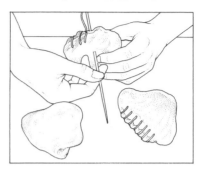

3 Use the stuffing to fill the
hearts and sew up neatly to
hold in the stuffing.

4 Chop the remaining onions
roughly. Heat the remaining
oil in a flameproof casserole, add
the hearts, carrot and chopped
onion and fry for about 5 minutes
until lightly browned.

5 Stir in the stock, tomato purée,
and salt and pepper. Bring to
the boil. Cover tightly and cook in
the oven at 170°C (325°F) mark 3
for 2½–3 hours, or until tender.
Serve the hearts whole or sliced
and pour the skimmed juices over.
Garnish with chopped parsley and
blanched julienne of lemon zest.

Menu Suggestion
Economical and filling, these
stuffed lamb's hearts make a
deliciously different family meal.
Serve with a colourful vegetable
macédoine and creamed potatoes.

**BAKED STUFFED LAMB'S
HEARTS**
Lamb's hearts vary in size quite
considerably, depending on the
time of year. Very young lamb's
hearts are small, weighing only
about 75 g (3 oz) each, whereas
the more mature hearts can
weigh as much as double this.
For this recipe, look for hearts
weighing around 150 g (5 oz)
each. Alternatively, if only the
small hearts are available, buy 6
and slice them before serving.

All Wrapped Up

In this chapter you will find an unusual selection of dishes in which meat is used as a filling. All of the recipes use a small quantity of meat in combination with other ingredients, and in each case the filling is 'wrapped up' in a variety of different ways. There are recipes from Britain, China, France, Greece, India, Italy and Mexico, each one illustrating how versatile lamb and pork can be.

PARMA CROISSANTS

$\boxed{0.50^*}$ 🥐 🥐 £ £ $\boxed{428\text{ cals}}$

* plus 30 minutes chilling

Serves 4

450 g (12 oz) Parma ham

1 egg, hard-boiled

200 g (7 oz) full-fat soft cheese

1 small garlic clove, skinned and crushed

pinch of ground cloves

salt and freshly ground pepper

212 g (7½ oz) packet frozen puff pastry, thawed

beaten egg, to glaze

fresh parsley sprigs, to garnish

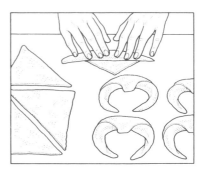

1 Finely chop 50 g (2 oz) of the ham and the egg. Place in a bowl with the cheese, garlic, cloves and salt and pepper to taste. Beat well together.

2 Roll out the pastry thinly on a lightly floured surface to a 30.5 cm (12 inch) square.

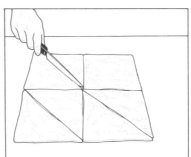

3 Cut into 4 squares, then halve each square to form 8 triangles.

4 Divide the cheese mixture between the triangles. Spread out a little towards the edges.

5 Roll up the pastries from the longest edge towards the opposite point and twist to form a croissant shape. Place on a wetted baking sheet and chill for 30 minutes.

6 Brush the croissants with beaten egg. Bake in the oven at 200°C (400°F) mark 6 for about 20 minutes, or until well risen and golden. Serve hot or just warm, garnished with parsley.

Menu Suggestion

Light and flaky Parma Croissants make a melt-in-the mouth starter for a dinner party. They are substantial enough to be served on their own, with a bottle of chilled white wine. Choose a dry, sparkling Asti Spumante from Italy, or a crisp, fruity Vinho Verde from Portugal.

PARMA CROISSANTS

Parma ham, correctly called *prosciutto di Parma* in Italian, is one of the world's great gastronomic delicacies—and one of the most expensive! Genuine Parma ham comes from around the town of Parma in Emilia-Romagna, northern Italy. By law, it must be dried for at least 8 months before being sold, although many Parma hams are dried for as long as 2 years, which gives them a wonderful smoky-sweet flavour.

BACON AND MUSHROOM PANCAKES

| 1.30 | 🏠 £ ✳* | 625 cals |

* freeze before baking at step 7

Serves 4

vegetable oil, for frying

one quantity pancake batter
  (page 156)

50 g (2 oz) butter or margarine

2 medium onions, skinned and
  roughly chopped

225 g (8 oz) cooked boiled bacon,
  finely chopped

175 g (6 oz) mushrooms, roughly
  chopped

30 ml (2 tbsp) plain flour

300 ml ($\frac{1}{2}$ pint) milk

125 g (4 oz) Cheddar cheese, grated

pinch of mustard powder

salt and freshly ground pepper

1 To make the pancakes, heat a
little oil in an 18 cm (7 inch)
heavy-based pancake or frying pan
until very hot, running it around
to coat the sides of the pan. Pour
off any surplus.

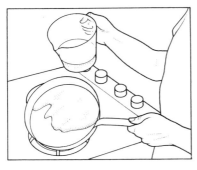

2 Ladle or pour in a little batter,
rotating the pan at the same
time, until enough batter is added
to give a thin coating.

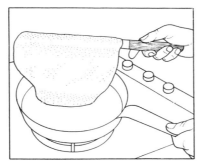

3 Cook until the pancake begins
to brown underneath. Ease a
palette knife under the centre and
flip over. Fry the other side until
golden brown, then turn on to a
warmed plate, cover with a sheet
of greaseproof paper and keep hot.
Continue cooking the batter to
make 8 pancakes, adding a little oil
to the pan each time. Stack the
pancakes up on the plate, interleaving each one with a sheet of
greaseproof paper.

4 Melt 25 g (1 oz) of the butter
in a deep frying pan, add the
onions and fry for about 5 minutes
until softened. Stir in the bacon
and mushrooms and fry 2–3
minutes until the mushrooms are
soft. Remove from the heat.

5 Melt the remaining 25 g (1 oz)
butter in a saucepan, add the
flour and cook gently, stirring, for
1–2 minutes. Remove from the
heat and gradually blend in the
milk. Bring to the boil, stirring
constantly, then simmer for 3
minutes until thick and smooth.
Add the cheese, mustard and salt
and pepper to taste and stir until
the cheese has melted. Remove
from the heat.

6 Fill the pancakes with the
bacon and mushroom filling
and roll or fold up. Place side by
side, seam side downwards, in a
buttered ovenproof dish.

7 Pour over the cheese sauce and
bake in the oven at 180°C
(350°F) mark 4 for 25–30 minutes.
Serve hot, straight from the dish.

Menu Suggestion

Serve these savoury pancakes for a
filling family supper dish.
Accompany them with a crisply
cooked green vegetable to give
contrast in texture and colour, or
with a mixed salad of grated raw
vegetables.

**BACON AND MUSHROOM
PANCAKES**

This dish is an excellent way to
make a meal out of a small
quantity of bacon leftover from a
joint which you have boiled
yourself. Alternatively, you can
use boiled ham, but do not buy
the ready-sliced variety as this
will be too thin. Ask for 'ham on
the bone' and get the shopkeeper
to carve a thick slice so that you
can chop it at home. If you
prefer to buy bacon especially to
make this dish, then the most
convenient way to buy it is in a
'boil-in-the-bag' vacuum pack.

BURRITOS

2.45	🍳	495 cals

Serves 6

450 g (1 lb) boneless pork shoulder

225 g (8 oz) beef stewing steak

vegetable oil, for frying

1 medium onion, skinned and chopped

1 garlic clove, skinned and finely chopped

5 ml (1 tsp) salt

5 ml (1 tsp) chilli powder

425 g (15 oz) can red kidney beans, drained

100 g (4 oz) Cheddar cheese, grated

12 hot tortillas (see page 156)

1 Trim the fat off the pork and beef, then cut the meat into 1 cm (½ inch) chunks.

2 Heat a little oil in a large saucepan, add the chunks of pork and beef a few at a time and brown them well, removing them with a slotted spoon as they brown.

3 Return all the meat to the pan. Add the onion, garlic, salt, chilli powder and 350 ml (12 fl oz) water. Bring to the boil, stirring.

4 Lower the heat, cover and simmer for 2 hours, or until the meat is so tender that it is beginning to fall apart.

5 When the meat is cooked, flake it with a fork. Continue cooking, uncovered, until the liquid has evaporated and the mixture has thickened.

6 Meanwhile, put the beans and cheese in a small saucepan and mix together. Stir over gentle heat until the cheese has melted.

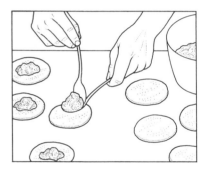

7 To make up a burrito, spread about 30 ml (2 tbsp) of the bean and cheese mixture over a tortilla, spoon about 30 ml (2 tbsp) of the meat mixture on top and fold the sides of the tortilla over. Serve hot.

Menu Suggestion
In Mexico, Burritos are eaten with the fingers, like tacos and tortillas. They make a filling lunch or supper dish, served with green pickled chillies (jalapeño), and ice-cold Mexican beer. In a traditional Mexican meal, Burritos are sometimes served as the 'dry soup' or *sopa seca*, after the first course 'wet' soup and before the main course—rather like the Italian pasta course.

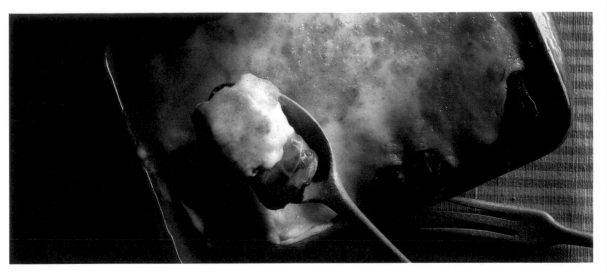

STUFFED CABBAGE ROLLS

| 1.45 | 🍲 £ ✳* | 658 cals |

* freeze at step 6, before baking

Serves 4

30 ml (2 tbsp) vegetable oil

1 medium onion, skinned and finely chopped

5 ml (1 tsp) chilli powder or to taste

350 g (12 oz) minced pork

225 g (8 oz) can tomatoes

salt and freshly ground pepper

283 g (10 oz) can red kidney beans, drained and rinsed

16 large leaves from a Savoy cabbage

450 ml ($\frac{3}{4}$ pint) coating cheese sauce (see page 157)

50 g (2 oz) mature Cheddar cheese, grated

pinch of cayenne or paprika, to finish

1 Heat the oil in a heavy-based saucepan, add the onion and fry gently for about 5 minutes until soft and lightly coloured. Sprinkle in the chilli powder and fry, stirring, for 1–2 minutes.

2 Add the pork and fry until browned, breaking up any lumps with a wooden spoon. Add the tomatoes with their juice and bring to the boil, stirring. Add salt and pepper to taste, then simmer over moderate heat for 20 minutes, stirring occasionally, until the pork is cooked and the sauce thick and well reduced. Stir in the kidney beans and remove from the heat.

3 Blanch the cabbage for 3 minutes, in batches of 4 leaves at a time, in a large pan of boiling salted water. Drain, rinse under cold running water and pat dry with absorbent kitchen paper.

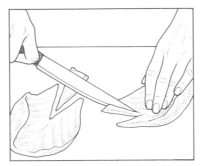

4 Lay the cabbage leaves flat on a board and cut out and discard the thick central stalks.

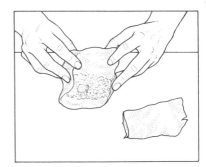

5 Put 15–25 ml (1–1½ tbsp) filling at the stalk end of each cabbage leaf. Fold the 2 sides inwards to cover the filling, then roll up to make a neat parcel.

6 Put the cabbage rolls, seam side down, in a single layer in a well-buttered baking dish. Pour the sauce into the dish. Cover and bake in the oven at 180°C (350°F) mark 4 for 30 minutes.

7 Sprinkle with the grated cheese and cayenne or paprika, and place under a preheated grill for about 5 minutes until golden brown and bubbling. Serve hot, straight from the dish.

Menu Suggestion
Stuffed Cabbage Rolls make a filling main course for a family meal. Serve with boiled rice.

SPRING ROLLS

| 1.00* | ▯ ▯ ✳* | 241 cals |

* plus 1 hour cooling; freeze at the end of step 7

Makes 8

225 g (8 oz) pork fillet or tenderloin

30 ml (2 tbsp) sesame or vegetable oil

2.5 cm (1 inch) piece of fresh root ginger, peeled and crushed

1 garlic clove, skinned and crushed

4 spring onions, trimmed and thinly sliced

100 g (4 oz) button mushrooms, roughly chopped

30 ml (2 tbsp) soy sauce

15 ml (1 tbsp) dark soft brown sugar

5 ml (1 tsp) five-spice powder

salt and freshly ground pepper

100 g (4 oz) beansprouts

beaten egg, for sealing

8 squares of spring roll pastry, thawed if frozen

vegetable oil, for deep-frying

spring onion tassels, to garnish

1 With a very sharp knife, cut the pork fillet into wafer thin, even-sized strips, discarding any fat and sinews.

2 Heat the oil in a wok or heavy-based frying pan, add the pork and stir-fry for about 10 minutes until just tender. Add the ginger and garlic and stir-fry over gentle heat for 2–3 minutes until lightly coloured.

3 Add the spring onions and mushrooms to the pan, increase the heat and stir-fry for a further 2–3 minutes, tossing the ingredients and shaking the pan constantly so that they colour evenly.

4 Mix the soy sauce, sugar and five-spice powder together. Add salt and pepper to taste, then stir into the pan. Add the bean-sprouts and toss to combine with the other ingredients for 1–2 minutes. Remove from the heat and leave to cool completely for about 1 hour.

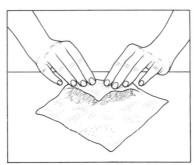

5 Brush beaten egg all over 1 square of pastry. Put one eighth of the filling in the corner nearest to you, then fold the corner over to cover the filling.

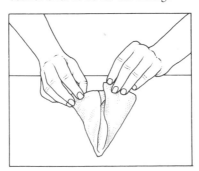

6 Fold in the corner at right angles to the first corner, then fold in the opposite corner.

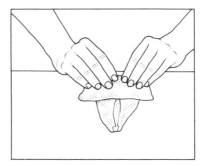

7 Roll up the filling in the pastry until the last corner is reached so that the filling is completely enclosed. Seal with a little beaten egg. Repeat with the remaining filling and 7 sheets of pastry.

8 Heat the oil in a deep-fat fryer to 180°C (350°F). Add the spring rolls and deep-fry in batches for 5 minutes until crisp and golden. Remove with a slotted spoon and drain on absorbent kitchen paper. Serve hot, garnished with spring onion tassels.

Menu Suggestion

Spring rolls are a traditional Chinese starter, which should be eaten with chopsticks. Serve them before a Chinese main course such as Sweet and Sour Pork (page 82) or Chinese Red-Cooked Pork (page 82).

SPRING ROLLS

These crisp, deep-fried pastries with their tasty Chinese filling of pork, mushrooms and beansprouts, are also sometimes called 'pancake rolls' in oriental restaurants. The special pastry needed for making them is sold in packets at oriental specialist shops. It is paper thin, but very easy to use, because it has been rolled and cut to the exact size required for making spring or pancake rolls. The packets of pastry will keep in the freezer for up to 3 months.

PORK CHOPS EN CROÛTE

1.30 | f | 788 cals

Serves 4

30 ml (2 tbsp) vegetable oil

15 g ($\frac{1}{2}$ oz) butter or margarine

4 pork loin chops

20 ml (4 tsp) chopped fresh sage or
  10 ml (2 tsp) dried sage

salt and freshly ground pepper

90 ml (6 tbsp) dry white wine or
  chicken stock

60 ml (4 tbsp) redcurrant jelly

400 g (14 oz) packet frozen puff
  pastry, thawed

beaten egg, to glaze

1 Heat the oil and butter in a
large, heavy-based frying pan,
add the chops in a single layer and
fry over moderate to high heat
until lightly browned on both
sides, turning once.

2 Lower the heat and sprinkle
the sage over the chops, with
salt and pepper to taste. Pour in
the wine or stock, then cover the
pan. Simmer the chops gently for
about 20 minutes or until almost
tender, basting frequently and
turning them once.

3 Remove the chops from the
pan and set aside to cool.
Meanwhile, stir the redcurrant
jelly into the pan juices and stir
over high heat to reduce and
combine. Remove from the heat.

4 Roll out the pastry on a
floured surface and cut out 4
squares, each one large enough to
enclose a pork chop.

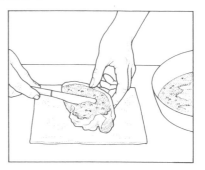

5 Place 1 chop in the centre of
each square of pastry and
spread with a little of the redcurrant jelly mixture.

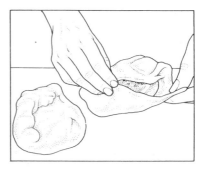

6 Wrap the pastry around the
chops, sealing the ends with
water. Place the parcels, seam side
down, on a wetted baking sheet.

7 Brush the parcels with beaten
egg to glaze, then decorate
with pastry trimmings, if liked,
and brush with more beaten egg.
Bake in the oven at 220°C (425°F)
mark 7 for about 20 minutes until
golden. Serve hot or cold, with the
remaining redcurrant jelly mixture.

Menu Suggestion
Loin pork chops encased in
crisp puff pastry can be served for
an everyday main course, but they
are special enough to be served
when entertaining guests. Suitable
accompaniments would be new
potatoes tossed in butter and
chopped fresh herbs, plus a mixed
salad of lettuce, radicchio,
cucumber and spring onions.

LAMB SAMOSAS

| 1.15* | | | 235 cals |

* plus 1 hour cooling

Makes 16

50 g (2 oz) ghee or butter

1 large onion, skinned and very finely chopped

1–2 garlic cloves, skinned and crushed

10 ml (2 tsp) ground coriander

10 ml (2 tsp) ground cumin

5 ml (1 tsp) turmeric

5 ml (1 tsp) chilli powder or to taste

450 g (1 lb) minced lamb

salt and freshly ground pepper

shortcrust pastry made with 225 g (8 oz) flour (page 157)

vegetable oil, for deep-frying

1 Make the filling. Melt the ghee or butter in a heavy–based saucepan, add the onion and garlic and fry for 5 minutes until soft.

2 Add the spices and continue frying, stirring constantly, for 1–2 minutes. Add the lamb and fry until well browned, breaking up any lumps with a wooden spoon.

3 Add salt and pepper to taste, then cook for a further 15–20 minutes until the mixture is quite dry. Stir frequently to prevent the lamb from catching on the bottom of the pan. Remove from the heat and leave to cool completely for about 1 hour.

4 Cut the pastry into 8 equal pieces. Roll out one piece on a well-floured surface to an 18 cm (7 inch) circle.

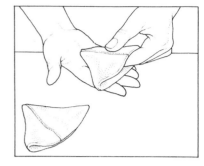

5 Cut the circle in half, pick up one half and form into a cone shape. Overlap the seam by 0.5 cm ($\frac{1}{4}$ inch) and seal with water.

6 Put 30–37.5 ml (2–2$\frac{1}{2}$ tbsp) filling inside the cone, then brush the open edges with water and press together to seal. Crimp or flute the sealed edge, if liked. Repeat with the remaining pastry and filling to make 16 samosas.

7 Heat the oil in a deep-fat fryer to 180°C (350°F). Add the samosas and deep-fry, a few at a time, for about 2 minutes until golden. Remove with a slotted spoon and drain on absorbent kitchen paper. Serve hot.

Menu Suggestion
Samosas make a delicious snack at any time of day. Serve them just as they are, or with a sauce made from natural yogurt, chopped fresh mint and cucumber. In India, samosas are eaten with the fingers as a snack food, but you can also serve them as a starter.

DOLMAS
(STUFFED VINE LEAVES)

| 2.45 | 🖐 £ | 309–464 cals |

Serves 4–6

225 g (8 oz) packet vine leaves
  preserved in brine

30 ml (2 tbsp) vegetable oil

1 medium onion, skinned and
  finely chopped

225 g (8 oz) minced lamb

30 ml (2 tbsp) tomato purée

150 ml ($\frac{1}{4}$ pint) natural yogurt

50 g (2 oz) long grain rice, boiled
  and drained

50 g (2 oz) pine nuts

45 ml (3 tbsp) chopped fresh mint

salt and freshly ground pepper

300 ml ($\frac{1}{2}$ pint) simple tomato
  sauce (page 158)

4 garlic cloves, skinned and cut
  into slivers

1 Soak the vine leaves in boiling water for 20 minutes, or according to packet instructions.

2 Meanwhile, heat the oil in a heavy-based saucepan, add the onion and fry gently for about 5 minutes until soft and lightly coloured. Add the lamb and fry until browned, breaking up any lumps with a wooden spoon.

3 Stir in the tomato purée and 60 ml (4 tbsp) of the yogurt and continue cooking and stirring for about 15 minutes until the mixture is dry.

4 Remove from the heat and stir in the rice, pine nuts, mint and plenty of salt and pepper. Set aside.

5 Drain the vine leaves and pat dry with absorbent kitchen paper. Place 1 vine leaf, vein side uppermost, flat on a board. Put a little filling at the base of the leaf.

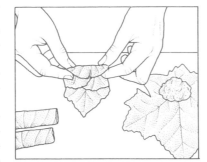

6 Fold the opposite sides of the leaf into the centre, then roll up around the filling like a cigar.

7 Squeeze the vine leaf gently in the palm of your hand to seal the parcel. Continue filling and rolling the leaves until all the filling and whole leaves are used up.

8 Put the ragged or torn vine leaves in the base of a large frying pan. Arrange the dolmas in a single layer on top, packing them tightly. Add the tomato sauce.

9 Push slivers of garlic down between the vine leaves. Cover with a lid and simmer very gently for 2 hours. Serve hot, or leave in the pan overnight and serve chilled on the following day. Drizzle the remaining yogurt over the dolmas just before serving.

Menu Suggestion
Dolmas are served cold as an appetizer in Greece, either on their own, or as part of the mixed hors d'oeuvre called *mezedhes* or *meze*, with small dishes of houmos (chick-pea and tahini dip), taramasalata (smoked cod's roe pâté), olives, and talattouri or tsatsiki (yogurt, cucumber and mint salad). They can also be served hot as a main course, with Greek sesame seed bread and a mixed salad of shredded lettuce, sliced onions and red and green peppers, quartered tomatoes and crumbled Feta cheese.

CHEESY SAUSAGE ROLLS

| 1.45 | £ ✳* | 143 cals |

* open freeze at step 8, before baking

Makes 20

225 g (8 oz) plain flour

2.5 ml (½ tsp) mustard powder

salt and freshly ground pepper

100 g (4 oz) butter or margarine

50 g (2 oz) Cheddar cheese, finely grated

15 ml (1 tbsp) vegetable oil

1 small onion, skinned and very finely chopped

20 ml (4 tsp) garam masala

225 g (8 oz) pork sausagemeat

beaten egg, to glaze

1 Make the pastry as page 157, sifting the mustard powder with the flour, salt and pepper, and adding the cheese before binding with 30 ml (2 tbsp) cold water.

2 Gather the dough together into a ball with one hand, then wrap in foil or cling film and chill for 30 minutes.

3 Meanwhile heat the oil in a small saucepan, add the onion and garam masala and fry gently for about 5 minutes until the onion is soft.

4 Put the sausagemeat in a bowl. Add the fried onion and mix well together. Divide the mixture into 2 equal halves and place on a floured surface.

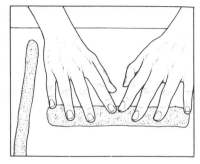

5 With your hands, roll and form each half into a sausage shape, 40.5 cm (16 inches) long.

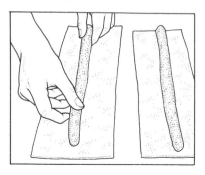

6 Divide the pastry into 2 equal halves and roll out each half into an oblong measuring 40.5 × 12.5 cm (16 × 5 inches). Place 1 roll of sausagemeat on each piece of pastry.

7 Fold the pastry over the sausagemeat to enclose it. Brush the long edge with water and press to seal.

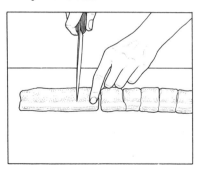

8 Cut each roll across into 10 lengths measuring 4 cm (1½ inches) each. Place on a baking sheet and brush with beaten egg to glaze. Bake in the oven at 190°C (375°F) mark 5 for 20–25 minutes until crisp and golden. Serve warm or cold.

Menu Suggestion

Serve these curry-flavoured Cheesy Sausage Rolls just as you would ordinary sausage rolls—for buffets, Christmas celebrations and packed lunches and picnics, or for a savoury snack or supper with hot soup.

Cold Pork Dishes

Sliced cold roast pork is a favourite meat for salads and sandwiches, but there are lots more interesting and unusual cold pork dishes, as this chapter illustrates. There are cold pastry dishes using pork, plus pâtés, meat loaves and Scotch eggs, as well as the famous British Raised Pork Pie, and the ever-popular cold gammon joint for buffets and parties.

SAUSAGE AND APPLE PLAIT

1.20 | f | ✳ | 592 cals

Serves 6

450 g (1 lb) pork sausagemeat
50 g (2 oz) fresh breadcrumbs
2 medium eating apples
2.5 ml ($\frac{1}{2}$ tsp) dried mixed herbs
salt and freshly ground pepper
370 g (13 oz) packet puff pastry, thawed
1 egg, beaten

1 In a large bowl, mix the sausagemeat and breadcrumbs. Peel 1 of the apples and grate into the sausagemeat mixture. Add the herbs and plenty of salt and pepper.

2 Roll out the pastry on a lightly floured surface to a 35.5 × 25.5 cm (14 × 10 inch) rectangle. Trim the edges if necessary.

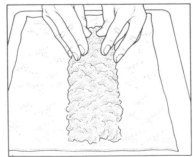

3 Place the pastry on a baking sheet. Put the sausagemeat down the centre, in a strip about 10 cm (4 inches) wide.

4 Peel, quarter, core and slice the remaining apple and arrange over the sausagemeat.

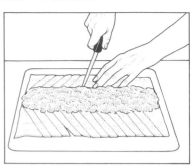

5 Using a sharp knife, cut the sides of the pastry into diagonal strips about 1 cm ($\frac{1}{2}$ inch) wide, cutting away from the edge of the sausagemeat.

6 Plait the strips of pastry to enclose the filling. Brush with beaten egg. Bake in the oven at 220°C (425°F) mark 7 for 35 minutes, covering lightly with foil after 20 minutes to prevent over-browning. Serve cold.

Menu Suggestion

Simple and economical to make, Sausage and Apple Plait is attractive when served whole for a buffet party or cold luncheon. Alternatively, wrap individual slices and pack in a lunch box or picnic hamper. Served hot, the plait makes the most delicious snack for lunch or supper.

SAUSAGE AND APPLE PLAIT

Apple and pork are a favourite combination, because the sweetness of apple cuts the richness of pork. In this case the combination works especially well, as sausagemeat in puff pastry tends to be very rich. If you use a tart eating apple such as a crisp Granny Smith's, this will also help counteract any fattiness in the pork and pastry, and give a good, sharp contrast of flavours.

RAISED PORK PIE

4.50* 🍳 🍳 **678 cals**

* plus 2 hours cooling, overnight
chilling and 1 hour setting

Serves 8

3–4 small veal bones

2 small onions, skinned

1 bay leaf

6 peppercorns

900 g (2 lb) boneless leg or shoulder
  of pork

1.25 ml ($\frac{1}{4}$ tsp) cayenne pepper

1.25 ml ($\frac{1}{4}$ tsp) ground mace

1.25 ml ($\frac{1}{4}$ tsp) ground ginger

1.25 ml ($\frac{1}{4}$ tsp) ground sage

1.25 ml ($\frac{1}{4}$ tsp) dried marjoram

salt and freshly ground pepper

1 quantity hot-water crust pastry
  (page 157)

beaten egg, to glaze

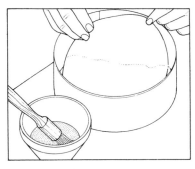

1 Grease and base-line a 20.5 cm
(8 inch) spring-release cake tin
with greaseproof paper.

2 Put the veal bones, onions, bay
leaf and peppercorns in a
saucepan and add water to cover.
Simmer for 20 minutes, then
bring to the boil and boil rapidly
until the liquid is reduced to
150 ml ($\frac{1}{4}$ pint). Strain the liquid
and leave to cool.

3 Meanwhile, cut the pork into
cubes. Put in a bowl with the
spices and herbs, 15 ml (3 tsp) salt
and pepper to taste. Mix well.

4 Prepare the hot-water crust
pastry as page 157. Knead for
3–4 minutes until smooth.

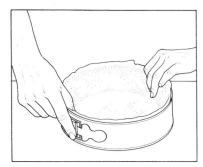

5 Roll out two-thirds of the
pastry on a lightly floured
surface and mould into the prepared tin. Cover and chill for 30
minutes. Cover the remaining
pastry with cling film or a damp
cloth and leave in a warm place.

6 Spoon the meat mixture and
60 ml (4 tbsp) of the cold stock
into the pastry case.

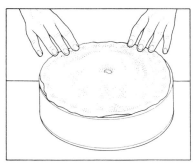

7 Roll out the reserved pastry
for the lid. Use to cover the
pie and seal the edge. Decorate
with the pastry trimmings. Make a
hole in the centre and brush with
beaten egg to glaze.

8 Bake in the oven at 220°C
(425°F) mark 7 for 30 minutes.
Cover loosely with foil, reduce the
oven temperature to 180°C
(350°F) mark 4 and bake for a
further 2$\frac{1}{2}$ hours. Leave the pie to
cool in the tin for 2 hours, then
chill overnight.

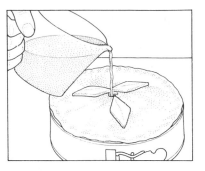

9 Warm the jellied stock to
liquefy and pour into the
centre of the pie. Chill for about 1
hour until set before serving.

Menu Suggestion

Raised Pork Pie is a classic for
picnics and buffets, and the
fact that it is home-made gives it
far more appeal than one bought
from a professional baker. Serve as
for any other pork pie, with a
selection of salads, pickles and
relishes. Fruity flavours such as
orange, apple, lemon and lime
help counteract the richness of the
meat and pastry, so try to include
these in your choice of salads,
which will also benefit from being
tossed in a sharp oil and vinegar
dressing rather than in a creamy
mayonnaise.

RICOTTA CHEESE AND HAM PIE

| 1.35* | £ £ ✳ | 491–736 cals |

* plus cooling

Serves 4–6

200 g (7 oz) shortcrust pastry
(page 157)

beaten egg, to glaze and seal

225 g (8 oz) Ricotta or cottage
cheese

225 g (8 oz) curd cheese

50 g (2 oz) Parmesan or Romano
cheese, grated

225 g (8 oz) cooked ham, diced

2 eggs

2.5 ml (½ tsp) dried oregano

salt and freshly ground pepper

1 Roll out two-thirds of the
pastry to a 25 cm (10 inch)
circle, about 0.3 cm (⅛ inch) thick.

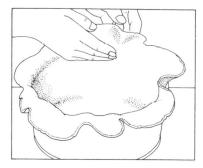

2 Line a 20.5 cm (8 inch) spring-
release cake tin with the pastry
circle. Trim the pastry to the top
edge of the tin and brush it with
some of the beaten egg to glaze.

3 Put the cheeses in a bowl
with the ham, eggs, oregano
and salt and pepper. Mix well.

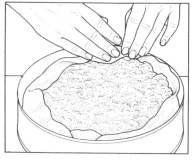

4 Spoon the mixture into the
pastry case and fold the edges
over the filling. Brush with more
beaten egg to glaze.

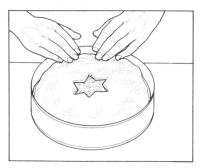

5 Roll out the remaining pastry
to a 20.5 cm (8 inch) circle and
cut a decorative design in it if you
wish. Place it over the filling,
sealing the edge by pressing
lightly on to the pastry below.
Brush the top with the remaining
beaten egg.

6 Bake in the oven at 190°C
(375°F) mark 5 for 1 hour or
until a knife inserted in the centre
comes out clean. Leave to cool
completely before cutting.

Menu Suggestion
This cold pie makes an excellent
summer lunch dish. The flavour
of the different cheeses is quite
strong, so salad accompaniments
should have definite flavours.
Fennel, chicory and spring onions
will all hold their own against the
sharpness of the cheese. Serve
with a robust red wine such as
a Chianti or Valpolicella.

PORK AND OLIVE PIE

2.20* 🍴 539 cals

* plus cooling and overnight chilling
Serves 6

225 g (8 oz) belly of pork
1 medium onion, skinned and
    quartered
225 g (8 oz) pork sausagemeat
2.5 ml ($\frac{1}{2}$ tsp) dried marjoram
salt and freshly ground pepper
175 g (6 oz) plain flour
75 g (3 oz) lard
24 stuffed green olives
beaten egg, to glaze

1 Pass the pork and onion through a mincer, fitted with the coarsest blade. Alternatively, chop in a food processor.

2 Put the minced mixture in a large bowl, add the sausage-meat, marjoram and salt and pepper to taste, then mix well together with your hands.

3 Put the flour into a separate bowl. Cut the lard into small pieces and add to the flour. Rub the lard into the flour until the mixture resembles fine bread-crumbs. Add about 45 ml (3 tbsp) water and bind to a firm dough.

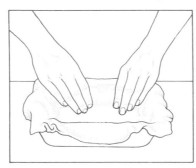

4 Roll out two-thirds of the pastry on a lightly floured surface and use to line the base and sides of a 1.7 litre (3 pint) loaf tin.

5 Fill the pastry case with the minced mixture, and the olives placed at intervals.

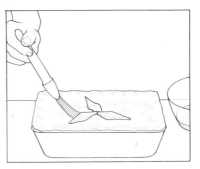

6 Roll out the remaining pastry for the lid. Use to cover the pie and seal the edges. Decorate with pastry trimmings and brush with beaten egg.

7 Bake in the oven at 200°C (400°F) mark 6 for about 40 minutes until well browned. Cover with foil, lower the oven temperature to 180°C (350°F) mark 4 and cook for a further 1 hour. Leave to cool, then chill overnight.

8 To serve, turn the pie out of the tin and leave at room temperature for 30 minutes.

Menu Suggestion
Pork and Olive Pie makes a rich cold lunch or supper dish, and is best served with a crisp green salad to provide a good contrast of colour and texture. Chilled dry cider would help offset the richness of the pie.

CHEESE AND BACON QUICHE

1.00* £ 602–903 cals

* plus at least 1 hour cooling

Serves 4–6

shortcrust pastry (page 157) made
    with 175 g (6 oz) flour and 40 g
    (1½ oz) butter or margarine and
    40 g (1½ oz) lard

50 g (2 oz) butter or margarine

1 large onion, skinned and finely
    chopped

4–6 streaky bacon rashers, rinded
    and chopped

10 ml (2 tsp) paprika

4 eggs, beaten

100 ml (4 fl oz) milk

100 g (4 oz) mature or farmhouse
    Cheddar cheese, grated

75 g (3 oz) Gruyère or Emmental
    cheese, grated

salt and freshly ground pepper

8 unsmoked bacon rashers

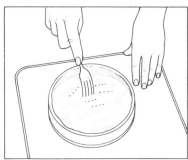

1 Roll out the pastry on a
floured surface and use to line
a 23 cm (9 inch) loose-bottomed
flan tin. Prick the base with a fork,
then line with foil and baking
beans. Bake blind in the oven at
190°C (375°F) mark 5 for 10
minutes, then remove the foil and
beans and return to the oven for a
further 5 minutes.

2 Meanwhile, make the filling.
Melt the butter in a saucepan,
add the onion, streaky bacon and
paprika and fry gently for 10
minutes. Turn into a bowl, add
the eggs, milk, Cheddar, 50 g (2 oz)
Gruyère, and salt and pepper to
taste and beat lightly.

3 Place the bacon under a preheated grill until lightly
cooked, then cut off the rinds.
Pour the cheese filling slowly into
the pastry case.

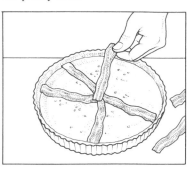

4 Arrange the bacon rashers in
the cheese filling, like the
spokes of a wheel. Sprinkle the
remaining Gruyère cheese in the
centre. Return the quiche to the
oven and bake for 20–25 minutes
until the filling is set. Leave to
cool for about 1 hour, then remove
from the tin to serve.

Menu Suggestion

Quiches are such versatile food.
They should always be served
warm or cold (never straight from
the oven), as the cooling allows
time for the filling to settle and the
flavours to mellow and mature.
The cheese and bacon flavours in
this quiche are quite strong, and
are best appreciated when served
with a simple salad—raw spinach
and mushroom or endive and
tomato would go especially well.

CHEESE AND BACON QUICHE

The paprika in this quiche gives
the cheese filling a lovely red
colour and a spicy, piquant
flavour. Look for the variety of
paprika labelled *süss*, which is
sweet and mild. Only buy it in
small quantities and store it in an
airtight container. Always check
the aroma of paprika before
using it, as it is a spice that can
quickly go musty.

COARSE LIVER PÂTÉ

3.20* ✳ 454 cals

* plus cooling and overnight chilling
Serves 8

225 g (8 oz) unsmoked rashers of
    streaky bacon, rinded

300 ml ($\frac{1}{2}$ pint) milk

slices of onion, bay leaf,
    peppercorns and 1 or 2 cloves,
    for flavouring

25 g (1 oz) butter or margarine

20 g ($\frac{3}{4}$ oz) plain flour

450 g (1 lb) belly of pork, rinded

450 g (1 lb) pig's liver

1 small onion, skinned and
    quartered

2 garlic cloves, skinned and
    crushed

30 ml (2 tbsp) medium dry sherry

salt and freshly ground pepper

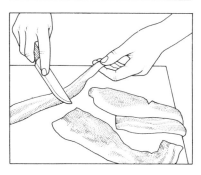

1 Put the bacon rashers on a board and stretch using the back of a knife. Use to line the base and sides of a 1.4 litre ($2\frac{1}{2}$ pint) dish or terrine.

2 Pour the milk into a saucepan, add the flavouring ingredients and bring slowly to the boil. Remove from the heat, cover and leave to infuse for 15 minutes.

3 Strain the milk and reserve. Melt the butter in the rinsed-out pan, add the flour and cook gently, stirring, for 1–2 minutes. Remove from the heat and gradually blend in the milk. Bring to the boil, stirring constantly, then simmer for 3 minutes until thick and smooth. Cover and leave to cool slightly.

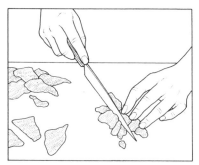

4 Cut the pork and liver into small pieces. Pass the meats and onion through a mincer, fitted with the coarsest blade. Alternatively, chop in a food processor.

5 Put the minced mixture into a bowl, add the garlic, then stir in the sherry and plenty of salt and pepper. Gradually beat in the cooled sauce and continue beating until well mixed. The mixture may seem a little sloppy, but it will firm up on cooking.

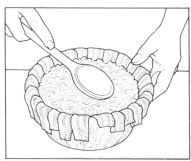

6 Spoon the mixture into the prepared dish and press down with the back of the spoon. Fold over any overlapping bacon. Cover the dish tightly with foil.

7 Place the dish in a roasting tin and half fill with boiling water. Bake in the oven at 180°C (350°F) mark 4 for about $2\frac{1}{4}$ hours until firm to the touch and the juices run clear when the centre of the pâté is pierced with a fine skewer.

8 Remove the dish from the roasting tin and replace the foil with a fresh piece. Place a plate or dish, small enough just to fit inside the dish, on top of the pâté. Top with heavy weights.

9 Leave the pâté to cool for 1 hour, then chill overnight. To serve, dip the dish into hot water for about 30 seconds then invert the pâté on to a plate.

Menu Suggestion
Coarse Liver Pâté makes a substantial starter for an informal supper party, served with salad, French bread and a full-bodied red wine such as a Côtes du Rhône. Alternatively, cut the pâté into thick slices and use for packed lunches and picnics, with a selection of salads.

MEAT LOAF

1.35*	✳	494–659 cals

*plus cooling and overnight chilling
Serves 6–8

900 g (2 lb) boneless leg or shoulder of pork, minced

225 g (8 oz) mushrooms, finely chopped

225 g (8 oz) streaky bacon, rinded and minced

2 medium onions, skinned and finely chopped

1 large garlic clove, skinned and crushed

125 g (4 oz) fresh breadcrumbs

150 ml ($\frac{1}{4}$ pint) soured cream

45 ml (3 tbsp) dry white wine

5 ml (1 tsp) dried mixed herbs

2.5 ml ($\frac{1}{2}$ tsp) ground allspice

1.25 ml ($\frac{1}{4}$ tsp) grated nutmeg

salt and freshly ground pepper

1 In a large bowl, mix all the ingredients together until evenly combined.

2 Pack the mixture into a 1.4 litre (2$\frac{1}{2}$ pint) loaf tin and cover with foil.

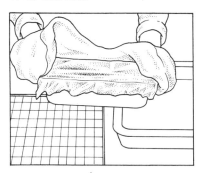

3 Half fill a roasting tin with water and place the loaf tin in the water bath. Cook in the oven at 190°C (375°F) mark 5 for 1 hour.

4 Uncover the tin, increase the oven temperature to 200°C (400°F) mark 6 and cook the meat loaf for a further 30 minutes.

5 Remove the tin from the water bath and leave to cool for 30 minutes. Cover with foil and place heavy weights on top. Chill in the refrigerator overnight.

6 To serve, turn the meat loaf out of the tin and cut into slices for serving.

Menu Suggestion
Thickly sliced Meat Loaf is similar to a pâté or terrine. Serve as a lunch dish with a potato or rice salad, and sprigs of watercress.

SPICY SCOTCH EGGS

0.40*	£	927 cals

* plus 30 minutes chilling

Makes 4

30 ml (2 tbsp) vegetable oil

1 onion, skinned and very finely chopped

10 ml (2 tsp) medium-hot curry powder

450 g (1 lb) pork sausagemeat

100 g (4 oz) mature Cheddar cheese, finely grated

salt and freshly ground pepper

4 eggs, hard-boiled

plain flour, for coating

1 egg, beaten

100–175 g (4–6 oz) dried breadcrumbs

vegetable oil, for deep-frying

1 Heat the 30 ml (2 tbsp) oil in a small pan, add the onion and curry powder and fry gently for 5 minutes until soft.

2 Put the sausagemeat and cheese in a bowl, add the onion and salt and pepper to taste. Mix with your hands to combine the ingredients well together.

3 Divide the mixture into 4 equal portions and flatten out on a floured board or work surface.

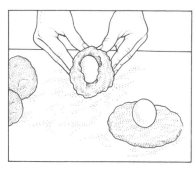

4 Place an egg in the centre of each piece. With floured hands, shape and mould the sausagemeat around the eggs. Coat lightly with more flour.

5 Brush each Scotch egg with beaten egg, then roll in the breadcrumbs until evenly coated. Chill for 30 minutes.

6 Heat the oil in a deep-fat fryer to 170°C (325°F). Carefully lower the Scotch eggs into the oil with a slotted spoon and deep-fry for 10 minutes, turning them occasionally until golden brown on all sides. Drain and cool on absorbent kitchen paper.

Menu Suggestion

Home-made Scotch eggs are quite delicious, with far more flavour than the commercial varieties. Serve them cut in halves or quarters with a mixed salad for lunch, or wrap them individually in cling film or foil and pack them for a picnic or packed lunch — they are easy to eat with the fingers. Scotch eggs can also be served hot for a family meal.

MEAT LOAF

The method of cooking meat loaves, pâtés and terrines in a roasting tin half filled with water is called '*au bain marie*' in French. It is a very simple method, but an essential one if the finished meat mixture is to be moist in texture. If the loaf tin is placed directly on the oven shelf, the mixture will dry out and the top will form a hard, unpleasant crust. A *bain marie* creates steam in the oven, which gives a moist heat. Special tins called water baths can be bought at kitchen shops for cooking '*au bain marie*', but an ordinary roasting tin does the job just as well.

PARTY GAMMON

| 3.00* | 533–665 cals |

* plus cooling

Serves 8–10

1.8 kg (4 lb) middle gammon joint

225 g (8 oz) mixed dried fruit
(prunes, figs, apricots)

juice of 1 orange

juice of 1 lemon

10 ml (2 tsp) ground mixed spice

60 ml (4 tbsp) honey

15 ml (1 tbsp) French mustard

about 30 Maraschino cherries and
60 long-stemmed cloves,
to garnish

1 Weigh the gammon and calculate the cooking time, allowing 25 minutes per 450 g (1 lb), plus 25 minutes. Put the gammon in a large saucepan and cover with cold water. Bring slowly to the boil, then drain off the water.

2 Cover the gammon with fresh cold water. Add the dried fruit, fruit juices and mixed spice and bring slowly to the boil again. Lower the heat, cover and simmer for the calculated cooking time.

3 Transfer the gammon to a roasting tin. Discard the cooking liquid, reserving the dried fruits. Strip the skin off the gammon while still hot, removing any string.

4 Mix together the honey and mustard and spread over the exposed fat of the gammon. Roast in the oven at 220°C (425°F) mark 7 for 10 minutes. Remove the gammon from the oven and leave until completely cold.

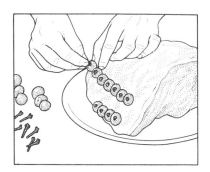

5 Cut each Maraschino cherry in half. Place the gammon on a serving platter and arrange the cherries over the glazed part, securing each one with a clove (see box). Surround with the reserved dried fruit, sliced if necessary. Serve cold.

Menu Suggestion

Party Gammon makes an attractive centrepiece for a cold table. Carve a few slices before serving, then let guests help themselves. Other dishes for a celebration cold table which would complement the gammon are potato salad, cold fish such as herrings or prawns in a creamy dressing, quiches and vol au vents, tomatoes stuffed with rice or Russian salad, a platter of sliced cold meats, sausages and salami, a selection of colourful and crisp salads, and baskets of different breads and rolls.

PARTY GAMMON

Glacé cherries can be used instead of Maraschino, but the latter have a far nicer flavour, and are more suitable for a special occasion. If you have difficulty in securing the cherry halves to the gammon with the cloves, use broken cocktail sticks and disguise the ends with cloves. Take great care to remove the sticks when slicing and serving the gammon.

Quick and Light Meals

Lamb and pork are such versatile meats, as this chapter illustrates so well. For midweek meals, try quick-cooking minced lamb and lean fillet, or pork escalopes, lamb's liver, pork chipolatas and ham. All the dishes in this chapter can be cooked in one hour or under, an absolute boon for busy cooks.

Minted Lamb Burgers with Cucumber

| 0.45 | £ | 381 cals |

Serves 4

450 g (1 lb) minced lamb

1 small onion, skinned and chopped

100 g (4 oz) fresh breadcrumbs

finely grated rind of $\frac{1}{2}$ lemon

45 ml (3 tbsp) chopped fresh mint

1 egg, beaten

salt and freshly ground pepper

30 ml (2 tbsp) plain flour

30 ml (2 tbsp) vegetable oil

$\frac{1}{2}$ cucumber

6 spring onions, trimmed

200 ml (7 fl oz) lamb or chicken stock

15 ml (1 tbsp) sherry

1 Mix the lamb, onion, bread-crumbs and lemon rind with 15 ml (1 tbsp) of the chopped mint, the beaten egg and salt and pepper to taste.

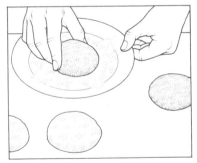

2 Shape into 12 flat burgers with floured hands and completely coat in the flour.

3 Heat the oil in a large frying pan, add the burgers and fry for about 6 minutes until lightly browned, turning once.

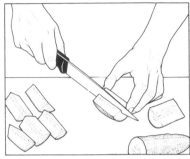

4 Cut the cucumber into 5 cm (2 inch) long wedges and the spring onions into 1 cm ($\frac{1}{2}$ inch) pieces. Add to the pan.

5 Pour in the stock and sherry, then add the remaining mint and salt and pepper to taste. Bring to the boil, cover the pan and simmer gently for about 20 minutes, or until the meat is tender. Skim off any excess fat before serving, and taste and adjust seasoning.

Menu Suggestion

The refreshing flavours of mint and cucumber in this dish go particularly well with new potatoes. Cook them in their skins to retain nutrients—and add extra flavour too.

MINTED LAMB BURGERS WITH CUCUMBER

Mint grows prolifically in any garden, and there are many different varieties to choose from. Spearmint is one of the most popular mints for cooking, especially with lamb, new potatoes and fresh garden peas. Applemint has a slight flavour of apples, as its name suggests; it has rounder, furrier leaves than spearmint, and makes excellent apple jelly and mint sauce. Peppermint is also easy to grow, and looks and tastes good if finely chopped and sprinkled over fruit salads; it also makes excellent tea.

LAMB AND PEPPER KEBABS

1.00* ✳* 404 cals

* plus 4 hours or overnight
marinating; freeze in the marinade
Serves 4

700 g (1½ lb) lamb fillet, trimmed
of fat

100 ml (4 fl oz) dry white wine

100 ml (4 fl oz) corn oil

50 ml (2 fl oz) lemon juice

2 celery sticks, trimmed and very
finely chopped

1 small onion, skinned and grated

2 garlic cloves, skinned and
crushed

1 large tomato, skinned and finely
chopped

20 ml (4 tsp) chopped fresh thyme
or 10 ml (2 tsp) dried thyme

salt and freshly ground pepper

1 medium red pepper

1 medium green pepper

few bay leaves

1 Cut the lamb into cubes and
place in a bowl. In a jug, whisk
together the wine, oil, lemon juice,
celery, onion, garlic, tomato,
thyme and salt and freshly ground
pepper to taste.

2 Pour the marinade over the
lamb and turn the meat until
well coated. Cover the bowl and
marinate in the refrigerator for
4 hours, preferably overnight.

3 When ready to cook, cut the
tops off the peppers and
remove the cores and seeds. Cut
the flesh into squares.

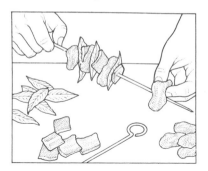

4 Remove the meat from the
marinade (reserving the
marinade) and thread on to 8 oiled
kebab skewers, alternating with the
squares of pepper and bay leaves.

5 Cook over charcoal or under a
preheated moderate grill for
20–25 minutes until the lamb is
tender. Turn the skewers
frequently during cooking and
brush with the reserved marinade.
Serve hot.

Menu Suggestion

For a really quick 'help-yourself'
type of meal, serve these kebabs in
pockets of hot pitta bread, and
accompany with bowls of
shredded lettuce or cabbage, sliced
tomato and cucumber.

LAMB AND PEPPER KEBABS

Lamb fillet is from the neck of
the animal. It is an excellent cut
for cutting into cubes for kebabs,
casseroles and curries, because it
is tender without being dry. Leg
of lamb can be boned and cubed,
but it is such a lean cut that it
tends to dry out on cooking.
Shoulder of lamb is also
sometimes boned and cubed, but
this tends to be more fatty and
sinewy. Many large
supermarkets sell lamb fillet, but
if you are buying it from a
butcher, you may have to order
in advance.

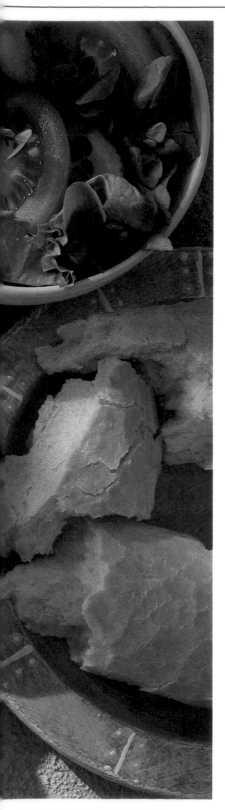

HAM AND CHEESE ROLLUPS

| 0.55 | £ £ | 437 cals |

Serves 4

30 ml (2 tbsp) olive oil

1 small onion, skinned and finely chopped

396 g (14 oz) can tomatoes

150 ml ($\frac{1}{4}$ pint) chicken stock

15 ml (1 tbsp) wine vinegar

5 ml (1 tsp) dried mixed herbs

5 ml (1 tsp) dried oregano or basil

pinch of sugar

salt and freshly ground pepper

8 slices (squares) of boiled ham

350–450 g ($\frac{3}{4}$–1 lb) cottage cheese with prawns, well drained (see box)

100 g (4 oz) Cheddar cheese, grated

fresh basil or parsley, to garnish

1 Make the tomato sauce. Heat the oil in a heavy-based saucepan, add the onion and fry gently for about 5 minutes until soft and lightly coloured.

2 Add the tomatoes with their juice and stir to break them up with a wooden spoon. Add the stock, wine vinegar, herbs, sugar and salt and pepper to taste. Bring to the boil, stirring. Lower the heat and simmer uncovered for 30 minutes, stirring occasionally.

3 Meanwhile, place 1 slice of ham flat on a board. Spoon one eighth of the cottage cheese along 1 edge of the ham and sprinkle with salt and pepper. Roll the ham up around the cheese.

4 Arrange the ham rolls, join side downwards, in a lightly buttered baking dish (or arrange 2 rolls in each of 4 individual gratin or baking dishes).

5 Pour over the tomato sauce and sprinkle evenly with the Cheddar cheese. Bake, uncovered, in the oven at 200 °C (400 °F) mark 6 for 10 minutes until golden and bubbling. Serve hot, garnished with basil or parsley.

Menu Suggestion

Serve for a tasty lunch or evening supper, with crusty French bread and a colourful side salad. For slimmers, make the tomato sauce without oil, use lean boiled ham, and Edam or Gouda cheese instead of the Cheddar.

HAM AND CHEESE ROLLUPS

Cottage cheese with prawns is available in cartons from most large supermarkets. Be sure to buy a reputable brand, however, because some brands are watery, with very few prawns. For this recipe the cottage cheese needs to be firm or the ham will not roll up successfully. As a precaution, drain the cheese in a fine sieve before use, pressing it with the back of a spoon to extract the whey. If you are feeling extravagant, add a few more peeled prawns to the cottage cheese. Drained and flaked tuna fish could also be used.

Most supermarkets sell packets of cheese slices, not only the processed cheese kind, but also Emmental, Gruyère, Samsoe and Havarti. These slices can be rolled up inside the ham, to give extra protein and flavour.

SPANISH PORK ESCALOPES

| 0.45 | £ £ | 347 cals |

Serves 4

450 g (1 lb) pork fillet or tenderloin
225 g (8 oz) tomatoes
15 ml (1 tbsp) vegetable oil
25 g (1 oz) butter or margarine
1 small onion, skinned and finely
  chopped
10 ml (2 tsp) plain flour
100 ml (4 fl oz) red wine
15 ml (1 tbsp) tomato purée
1 garlic clove, skinned and crushed
salt and freshly ground pepper
12 stuffed green olives, sliced

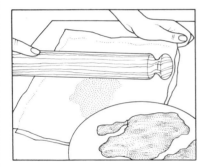

1 Cut the pork into 8 pieces
and bat out thinly between
sheets of non-stick paper.

2 Skin and quarter the tomatoes.
Put the seeds into a sieve
resting over a bowl and press
through and reserve the juices.
Discard the seeds and roughly
chop the flesh.

3 Heat the oil and butter in a
large frying pan, add half of
the pork and fry until browned
on both sides. Remove from the
pan with a slotted spoon and set
aside. Repeat with remaining pork.

4 Add the onion to the pan and
fry for about 5 minutes until
lightly browned. Stir in the flour
and cook for 1 minute, then
gradually add the wine, chopped
tomatoes and their juice, the
tomato purée, garlic and salt and
pepper to taste. Bring to the boil,
stirring all the time.

5 Return the meat to the pan.
Add the sliced olives, cover
and simmer for 10–15 minutes or
until the pork is tender. Serve hot.

Menu Suggestion
With their tomato and wine sauce,
these pork escalopes need an
accompaniment that will soak up
the juices. Serve with risotto rice,
which can be cooked at the same
time, then follow with a salad.

**SPANISH PORK
ESCALOPES**

There are two quick and easy
ways to skin tomatoes. The best
method for firm tomatoes is to
put them in a large bowl and
pour over boiling water. Leave
for 10 seconds, then drain and
plunge into a bowl of cold water.
Remove the tomatoes from the
water one at a time, make a tiny
cut in the skin with the point of a
sharp knife, then peel off the skin
with your fingers. If you only
have to deal with one or two ripe
tomatoes and have a gas hob, the
following method is very simple
and quick. Pierce the tomato in
the stalk end with the prongs of a
fork, then hold the tomato in the
flames and turn it constantly
until the skin blisters and bursts.
Leave until cool enough to
handle, then the skin will peel
away easily.

STIR-FRIED PORK AND VEGETABLES

0.50	433 cals

Serves 4

700 g (1½ lb) pork fillet or tenderloin, trimmed of fat

60 ml (4 tbsp) dry sherry

45 ml (3 tbsp) soy sauce

10 ml (2 tsp) ground ginger

salt and freshly ground pepper

1 medium cucumber

30 ml (2 tbsp) vegetable oil

1 bunch of spring onions, trimmed and finely chopped

1–2 garlic cloves, skinned and crushed (optional)

30 ml (2 tbsp) cornflour

300 ml (½ pint) chicken stock

175 g (6 oz) beansprouts

1 Cut the pork in thin strips and place in a bowl. Add the sherry, soy sauce, ginger and salt and pepper to taste, then stir well to mix. Set aside.

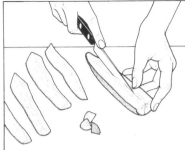

2 Prepare the cucumber sticks. Cut the cucumber in half, then cut into quarters lengthways, discarding the rounded ends. Leave the skin on, to add colour.

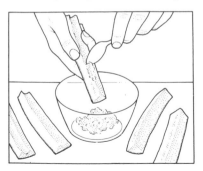

3 Using a sharp-edged teaspoon, scoop out the seeds and discard. Cut the cucumber quarters lengthways again, then slice across into strips about 2.5 cm (1 inch) long.

4 Heat the oil in a wok or large, heavy-based frying pan, add the spring onions and garlic, if using, and fry gently for about 5 minutes until softened.

5 Add the pork to the pan, increase the heat and stir-fry for 2–3 minutes until lightly coloured, tossing constantly so that it cooks evenly.

6 Mix the cornflour with the cold chicken stock and set aside.

7 Add the cucumber, spring onions and beansprouts to the pork, with the cornflour and stock. Stir-fry until the juices thicken and the ingredients are well combined. Taste and adjust seasoning, then turn into a warmed serving dish. Serve immediately.

Menu Suggestion

Both meat and vegetables are cooked together in this Chinese-style dish. For a simple meal, serve on a bed of egg noodles or plain boiled rice.

CHIPOLATAS AND BEANS

| 0.30 | £ | 639 cals |

Serves 4

30 ml (2 tbsp) vegetable oil

450 g (1 lb) pork chipolata sausages

1 large onion, skinned and sliced

4 rashers of streaky bacon, rinded and chopped

430 g (15 oz) can red kidney beans, drained

150 ml ($\frac{1}{4}$ pint) beef stock

salt and freshly ground pepper

chopped fresh parsley, to garnish

1 Heat the oil in a flameproof casserole, add the sausages and fry until browned on all sides. Remove the sausages from the pan with a slotted spoon and set aside.

2 Add the onion and bacon to the pan and fry about 5 minutes, stirring occasionally, until they begin to turn brown.

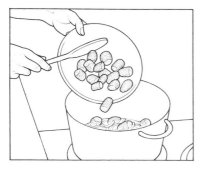

3 Cut each sausage into 4 and return to the pan with the kidney beans, beef stock and salt and pepper to taste. Cover and cook gently for about 15 minutes, or until the sausages are tender. Serve hot, garnished with parsley.

Menu Suggestion

Serve Chipolatas and Beans for a quick family supper, with mashed potatoes or jacket baked potatoes. Alternatively, for a nourishing snack, serve on buttered wholemeal or granary toast.

LIVER STROGANOFF

0.30	£	321 cals

Serves 4

4 thin slices of lamb's liver, total weight 350 g (12 oz)

25 g (1 oz) butter or margarine

1 medium onion, skinned and thinly sliced

225 g (8 oz) button mushrooms, thinly sliced

15 ml (1 tbsp) tomato purée

10 ml (2 tsp) Dijon-style mustard

30 ml (2 tbsp) brandy

salt and freshly ground pepper

150 ml ($\frac{1}{4}$ pint) soured cream, at room temperature

chopped fresh parsley, to garnish

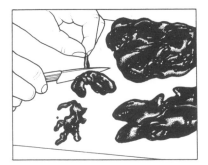

1 Slice the liver into thin strips, cutting off and discarding any ducts and gristle. Melt the butter in a large, heavy-based frying pan, add the liver and fry over moderate heat for about 5 minutes, stirring constantly and tossing the pan so that the strips become evenly and lightly coloured. Remove with a slotted spoon and set aside.

2 Add the sliced onion to the pan and fry over a moderate heat for about 5 minutes until soft but not coloured. Remove the onion from the pan with a slotted spoon and add to the liver.

3 Add the mushrooms to the pan, increase the heat and toss until the juices run. Remove and add to the liver and onions.

4 Stir the tomato purée and mustard into the pan juices, then the brandy. Stir over high heat, scraping up the sediment from the base of the pan.

5 Return the liver, onion and mushrooms to the pan and stir to combine with the juices. Add salt and pepper to taste, then remove from the heat.

6 Whisk the soured cream vigorously, then stir about half into the stroganoff. Turn the stroganoff into a warmed serving dish and drizzle with the remaining soured cream. Sprinkle with chopped parsley and serve.

Menu Suggestion

Tagliatelle noodles go well with stroganoff. Follow with a colourful mixed salad such as red and green pepper rings, lettuce and avocado. Salad or 'cocktail' avocados have no stones, and are very quick and easy to prepare.

Classic Dishes

Some of the best lamb and pork dishes are the classic, time-honoured favourites, and in this chapter you will find a wide cross-section of traditional meat dishes from all over the world. Some are for entertaining, some for everyday family meals. Whichever you choose, you will find them all equally delicious.

IRISH STEW

| 2.20 | £ | ✳ | 318 cals |

Serves 4

700 g (1½ lb) middle neck of lamb

2 medium onions, skinned and sliced

450 g (1 lb) old potatoes, peeled and thinly sliced

15 ml (1 tbsp) chopped fresh parsley, plus extra to garnish

5 ml (1 tsp) dried thyme

salt and freshly ground pepper

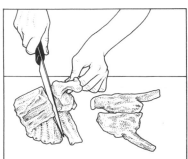

1 Cut the meat into cutlets, and trim away any excess fat or gristle with a sharp knife.

2 Make layers of meat and vegetables in a deep casserole, sprinkling each layer with parsley, thyme and salt and freshly ground pepper to taste.

3 Finish with a top layer of potato to make a neat 'lid'. Pour 300 ml (½ pint) water slowly into the casserole.

4 Cover with greaseproof paper or foil, then the casserole lid. Bake in the oven at 170°C (325°F) mark 3 for about 2 hours, or until the meat feels tender and the vegetables soft when pierced with a skewer. Serve very hot, garnished with the extra parsley.

Menu Suggestion

Irish Stew is a traditional family dish. Serve with colourful vegetables such as carrots, peas, Brussels sprouts or beans.

IRISH STEW

This is a traditional recipe for Irish Stew, in which only meat, potatoes, onions, herbs and seasonings are used. Nowadays, sophisticated cooks tend to spoil the pure flavour of Irish Stew by adding carrots, turnips and pearl barley, in the mistaken belief that the traditional dish is too plain and homely. Irish Stew was originally a farmers' dish, and only ingredients raised or grown on the farm were included in it.

Original recipes used goat or mutton—the long, slow cooking tenderised the tough meat. Lamb in the form of best end or middle neck chops are now used, with equally good results. If liked, you can arrange these chops around the edge of the casserole with their bones pointing upwards, then layer the other ingredients in the centre. This method looks attractive and makes the stew very easy to serve.

MOUSSAKA

| 1.40* | 🍴 £ ❊* | 632–948 cals |

* plus 30 minutes to dégorge the aubergines and 15 minutes standing; freeze before baking at step 8

Serves 4–6

2 medium aubergines

salt and freshly ground pepper

about 150 ml (¼ pint) olive or vegetable oil, or a mixture of both

1 large onion, skinned and roughly chopped

1–2 garlic cloves, skinned and crushed

450 g (1 lb) minced lamb

227 g (8 oz) can tomatoes

30 ml (2 tbsp) tomato purée

10 ml (2 tsp) dried oregano

5 ml (1 tsp) ground allspice

2 bay leaves

410 g (14½ oz) can evaporated milk

40 g (1½ oz) cornflour

25 g (1 oz) butter or margarine

25 g (1 oz) plain flour

pinch of grated nutmeg

1 egg, beaten

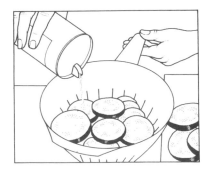

1 Slice the aubergines thinly and place in a colander, sprinkling each layer with salt. Cover with a plate, place heavy weights on top and leave the aubergines to dégorge for 30 minutes.

2 Meanwhile, heat 30 ml (2 tbsp) of the oil in a heavy-based saucepan, add the onion and garlic and fry gently for 5 minutes until soft and lightly coloured. Add the minced lamb and fry until well browned, stirring and pressing with a wooden spoon to break up any lumps.

3 Add the tomatoes with their juice, the tomato purée, oregano, allspice and salt and pepper to taste, then add the bay leaves. Cover and simmer for about 20 minutes, stirring occasionally to break up the tomatoes.

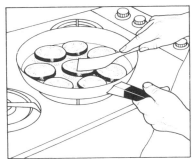

4 Meanwhile, rinse the aubergines under cold running water, then pat dry with absorbent kitchen paper. Pour enough oil into a heavy-based frying pan to just cover the base. Heat until very hot, then add a layer of aubergine slices. Fry until golden on both sides, turning once, then remove with a spatula and drain on absorbent kitchen paper. Continue frying and draining all the aubergine slices in this way, adding more oil to the pan as necessary.

5 Make the sauce for the topping. Dilute the evaporated milk with water to make up to 1 litre (1¾ pints) as directed on the can. In a jug, mix the cornflour to a smooth paste with a few spoonfuls of the milk.

6 Melt the butter in a saucepan, add the flour and cook gently, stirring, for 1–2 minutes. Remove from the heat and gradually blend in the milk. Bring to the boil, stirring constantly, then simmer for 3 minutes.

7 Stir in the cornflour paste and continue simmering and stirring until the sauce is thick. Remove the pan from the heat, add the nutmeg and salt and pepper to taste, then stir in the beaten egg.

8 Arrange the meat and aubergines in layers in a baking dish, then pour over the sauce. Bake, uncovered, in the oven at 180°C (350°F) mark 4 for 40 minutes. Leave to stand at room temperature for at least 15 minutes before serving.

Menu Suggestion

Greek Moussaka is an extremely filling dish. Serve for a family meal, or even for an informal supper party, with Greek sesame seed bread and a mixed salad. Retsina wine is the ideal drink to accompany Greek food.

SHEFTALIA
(CYPRIOT SAUSAGE KEBABS)

| 0.25* | 🍳 | ✳* | 277–415 cals |

* plus 30 minutes chilling; freeze after shaping in step 3

Serves 4–6

450 g (1 lb) boneless leg or shoulder of lamb, minced

225 g (8 oz) belly of pork, rinded

1 large onion, skinned

60 ml (4 tbsp) chopped parsley

salt and freshly ground pepper

lemon wedges, to serve

1 Put the lamb in a large bowl. Cut the pork into small pieces and the onion into quarters. Pass the pork and onion through a mincer into the bowl with the lamb. Alternatively, finely chop all the ingredients in a food processor. Add the parsley and salt and pepper to taste.

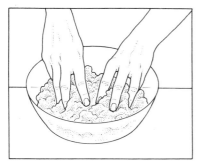

2 Knead the mixture thoroughly with your fingers until it is smooth and well mixed.

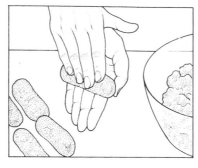

3 With damp hands, shape into 12 sausage shapes about 5 cm (2 inches) long. Thread on to 4–6 flat metal skewers. Chill in the refrigerator for 30 minutes.

4 Cook over a charcoal barbecue or under a preheated grill for about 15 minutes until cooked, turning frequently. Serve hot, with lemon wedges.

Menu Suggestion

Sheftalia are usually served with pitta bread and rice for an informal meal. A typical Cypriot mixed salad to accompany these kebabs would be a combination of tomatoes, raw onions, lettuce, cucumber and large black olives, tossed in an oil and vinegar dressing with plenty of chopped fresh mint.

SHEFTALIA

In Cyprus, Sheftalia are wrapped in caul before cooking; this melts away and makes the meat moist and juicy. Caul, which is the fatty membrane from the stomach of a pig or sheep, is available from family butchers, and is well worth buying to make these sausage kebabs more authentic. Before use, soak the caul for 20–30 minutes in tepid water to which a splash of vinegar or lemon juice has been added. This softens and separates the caul and makes it easier to manage; dry caul tends to tear easily. Drain after soaking, then cut into pieces which are large enough to encase the sausage mixture. Simply place the mixture along one edge of a piece of caul, then roll the caul up around it, tucking in the ends as you roll.

LANCASHIRE HOT POT

| 2.40 | £ | ✳ | 427 cals |

Serves 4

8 middle neck lamb chops

2 lamb's kidneys

8 shelled oysters (optional—see box)

2 medium onions, skinned and sliced

125 g (4 oz) mushrooms, sliced

5 ml (1 tsp) dried thyme

salt and freshly ground pepper

450 g (1 lb) potatoes, peeled and thinly sliced

450 ml ($\frac{3}{4}$ pint) lamb or beef stock

25 g (1 oz) lard or dripping

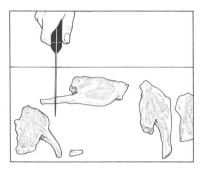

1 Remove any excess fat from the lamb. Select a large, deep casserole. If it is not deep enough to hold the meat, chop the ends off the bones.

2 Skin, halve and core the kidneys and divide each half into 3–4 pieces.

3 Layer the meat in the casserole with the oysters, if using, the kidneys, onions and mushrooms. Sprinkle each layer with thyme and salt and pepper to taste. If the casserole has a narrow top, add some of the potatoes at this stage. Pour in the stock.

4 Arrange a layer of overlapping potato slices on top. Melt the lard and brush over the potatoes. Cover and cook in the oven at 170°C (325°F) mark 3 for 2 hours, or until both the meat and the potatoes are tender when tested with a skewer.

5 Remove the lid carefully, increase the oven temperature to 220°C (425°F) mark 7 and continue cooking for about 20 minutes, or until the potatoes are golden brown and crisp. Serve hot.

Menu Suggestion

Lancashire Hot Pot makes a filling family meal. It is especially good in cold weather, with a nourishing vegetable dish like 'mushy' peas or mashed root vegetables. Pickled red cabbage was the traditional accompaniment, but ordinary red cabbage tastes just as good.

LANCASHIRE HOT POT

One of the best known of Lancashire dishes, the hot pot takes its name from the tall earthenware dish in which it was traditionally cooked. The long boned chops from the Pennine sheep could be stood vertically around the pot and the centre filled with vegetables, kidneys, mushrooms and, in the days when they were cheap, oysters. A thatch of sliced potatoes completed the dish.

LAMB CUTLETS REFORM

1.15 | 🍳 | £ £ | 643 cals

Serves 4

50 g (2 oz) butter or 60 ml (4 tbsp) vegetable oil plus extra for frying

1 small onion, skinned and finely chopped

1 medium carrot, peeled and finely chopped

50 g (2 oz) lean uncooked ham, finely diced

60 ml (4 tbsp) red wine vinegar

45 ml (3 tbsp) port

600 ml (1 pint) lamb or chicken stock

30 ml (2 tbsp) redcurrant jelly

2 cloves

2 blades of mace

1 bay leaf

4 juniper berries, crushed

a pinch of dried thyme

8 lamb cutlets

50 g (2 oz) cooked ham, finely minced

50 g (2 oz) fresh white breadcrumbs

1 egg, size 2, beaten

15 ml (1 tbsp) cornflour

1 hard-boiled egg white, cut into fine strips

1 slice of cooked tongue, cut into fine strips

1 gherkin, cut into fine strips

2 button mushrooms, finely sliced

salt and freshly ground pepper

cutlet frills, to serve

1 Make the Reform sauce. Melt the butter in a medium, heavy-based saucepan, add the onion, carrot and diced uncooked ham and cook gently until just turning brown. Add the vinegar and port and boil rapidly until almost all the liquid evaporates.

2 Remove the pan from the heat and add the stock, redcurrant jelly, cloves, mace, bay leaf, juniper and thyme. Stir well, return to the heat and bring to the boil. Lower the heat and simmer gently for about 30 minutes.

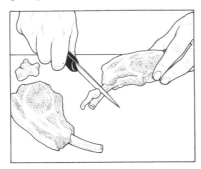

3 Meanwhile, trim the cutlets to remove most of the surrounding fat. Scrape the bone absolutely clean, to within 2.5 cm (1 inch) of the 'eye' of the meat.

4 Mix the minced ham and breadcrumbs together. Brush each cutlet with beaten egg and coat with the ham and bread-crumb mixture. Cover and chill until required.

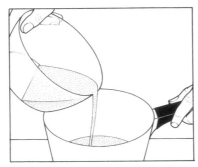

5 Strain the sauce through a fine sieve and return to the rinsed-out saucepan. Blend the cornflour with about 30 ml (2 tbsp) water and add to the sauce. Stir well and bring the sauce to the boil, stirring continuously. Simmer until thickened, then add the strips of egg white, tongue and gherkin, and the mushroom slices. Season and remove from the heat.

6 Heat about 60 ml (4 tbsp) oil or butter in a large, heavy-based frying pan, add the cutlets and fry gently for about 4 minutes on each side until golden brown. Remove from the pan and drain on absorbent kitchen paper.

7 Arrange the cutlets on a warmed serving dish and garnish each one with a cutlet frill. Reheat the sauce gently and serve separately.

Menu Suggestion

Serve classic Lamb Cutlets Reform for an elegant dinner party main course, with side plates of crisply cooked vegetables in nouvelle-cuisine style. Whole young carrots, mange-touts and French beans would all go very well.

LAMB CUTLETS REFORM

Reform Sauce to serve with lamb cutlets or chops was invented in the 1830s by the great French chef Alexis Soyer. At that time, Soyer was Chef de Cuisine at the Reform Club in London's Pall Mall, and he created the recipe specially for the club's members. The Reform Club was founded by liberal politicians after the Great Reform Bill of 1832, as a meeting place for politicians after parliament. It is still in Pall Mall, and Lamb Cutlets Reform continues to be a popular item on the menu with today's politicians. One of the original ways to serve the dish was to arrange the cutlets on a large platter in the shape of a wreath, then to place the garnish in the centre. In this case, the brown sauce was served separately in a sauceboat.

TOAD IN THE HOLE

| 0.45 | £ | 483–643 cals |

Serves 3–4

450 g (1 lb) pork sausages
25 g (1 oz) lard or dripping
225 ml (8 fl oz) milk
100 g (4 oz) plain flour
pinch of salt
1 egg

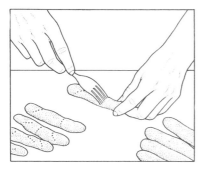

1 Prick the sausages all over with a fork. Put the lard in a Yorkshire pudding tin or small roasting tin and add the sausages.

2 Bake in the oven at 220°C (425°F) mark 7 for 10 minutes until the lard is hot.

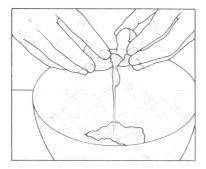

3 Meanwhile, make the batter. Mix the milk and 50 ml (2 fl oz) water together in a jug. Put the flour and salt in a bowl. Make a hollow in the centre and break the egg into it.

4 Mix the flour and egg together gradually, then add the milk and water, a little at a time, and beat until the mixture is smooth.

5 Pour the batter into the tin. Bake for about 30 minutes, or until golden brown and well risen. Do not open the oven door during baking or the batter might sink. Serve at once.

Menu Suggestion
Serve for an everyday family supper, with a crisply cooked green vegetable. Children will probably like Toad in the Hole with baked beans, which are just as nutritious as green vegetables.

TOAD IN THE HOLE
One of northern England's most famous dishes, Toad in the Hole is simply a Yorkshire pudding batter cooked with pork sausages. Years ago in Victorian times, when larger quantities of meat were eaten than they are today, Toad in the Hole was made with rump steak. Some cooks even added oysters and mushrooms to the steak, and there is even a recipe for Toad in the Hole made with a boned, stuffed chicken! Kidneys were also a favourite ingredient in those days and, if you like their flavour, they make a good combination with the sausages. You will need about 3 lamb's kidneys, which should be sliced and cooked with the sausages before pouring in the batter.

DAUBE D'AGNEAU
(FRENCH BRAISED LAMB)

4.05* £ £ 610 cals

* plus overnight marinating

Serves 6

1.4 kg (3 lb) leg of lamb

600 ml (1 pint) red wine

1 medium onion, skinned and chopped

3 medium carrots, peeled and diced

5 sprigs of parsley

2 sprigs of thyme

1 bay leaf

salt and freshly ground pepper

75 ml (5 tbsp) olive oil

225 g (8 oz) salt pork

1 pig's trotter, split (optional)

2 garlic cloves, skinned and crushed

4 firm red tomatoes, skinned, quartered and seeded

1 Put the lamb in a large, heavy-gauge polythene bag, or in 1 thin bag inside another. Place it in a large bowl and put into the bag the wine, onion, carrots, herbs and salt and pepper to taste. Pour in the olive oil and seal the bag.

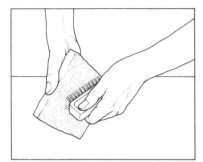

2 Scrub the rind of the salt pork. Put it in a pan with the pig's trotter, if using. Cover with water, bring to the boil, then drain and cover with fresh cold water. Leave both the lamb and the pork in a cool place overnight.

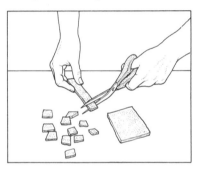

3 The next day, drain the pork and pig's trotter, if used. Cut the rind off the pork and scissor-snip it into small squares. Cut the flesh into narrow strips.

4 Put the lamb and its marinade in a deep casserole. Add the pork, the pig's trotter, if used, the garlic and 2 of the tomatoes. Cover tightly and cook in the oven at 170°C (325°F) mark 3 for about 3½ hours. Baste the joint occasionally.

5 Transfer the lamb to a warmed serving platter and keep hot. Skim the surface fat from the juices. Strain the diced vegetables and spoon them around the joint.

6 Boil the pan juices until reduced one quarter, then pour them over the meat. Garnish with the remaining tomato quarters. Serve hot.

Menu Suggestion

Daube d'Agneau is a French country-style dish, which makes an excellent family meal. Serve with boiled or steamed potatoes tossed in melted butter and chopped fresh mint or parsley. Follow with French beans or a tossed green salad.

DAUBE D'AGNEAU

The French word *daube* comes from *daubière*, the name for a covered casserole. Daubes are made by country cooks all over France, but particularly in the region of Provence. Ingredients vary enormously from one cook to another, but the dish is essentially homely in style. Wine is always included, and the meat is first marinated, then cooked long and slow in the oven. Sometimes beef is used rather than the lamb suggested here, and sometimes the meat is sliced or cubed, especially if it is a tough, sinewy cut.

KIBBEH

(MIDDLE EASTERN LAMB AND CRACKED WHEAT PATTIES)

| 1.30 | ▯ ▯ ✳* | 449–748 cals |

* freeze before deep-frying

Serves 4–6

700 g (1½ lb) minced lamb

1 onion, skinned and roughly chopped

225 g (8 oz) cracked wheat (burghul)

salt and freshly ground pepper

vegetable oil, for deep-frying

25 g (1 oz) pine nuts

30 ml (2 tbsp) chopped fresh parsley

1.25 ml (¼ tsp) ground allspice

lemon wedges, to serve

1 Put 550 g (1¼ lb) of the lamb in a blender or food processor with the onion. Work to a smooth, paste-like consistency. (Or work several times through a mincer, fitted with the finest blade.)

2 Put the cracked wheat in a sieve and rinse under cold running water. Turn on to a clean tea towel and wring out as much moisture as possible.

3 Add the wheat to the meat mixture and work again in the machine (or mincer). Add salt and pepper to taste and set aside.

4 Make the filling. Heat 30 ml (2 tbsp) of the oil in a saucepan. Add the pine nuts and fry until browned, shaking the pan and tossing the nuts constantly. Remove with a slotted spoon. Add remaining minced lamb to the pan and fry until browned. Cook gently for 15 minutes, stirring frequently. Remove from the heat and stir in the pine nuts, parsley, allspice and salt and pepper.

5 With wet hands, take a small piece of the wheat and meat mixture, about the size of an egg. Hold it in one hand and, with the index finger of the other, make an indent in the centre.

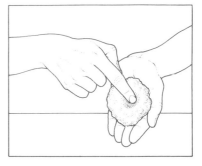

6 Work the kibbeh round in your hand, pressing down with the index finger until the hole in the centre is quite large and the kibbeh is oval or 'torpedo' shaped.

7 Put about 5 ml (1 tsp) of the filling in the centre of the kibbeh, then close the kibbeh around it, wetting the mixture to seal. Roll the kibbeh between wetted palms to ensure a smooth shape, sealing any cracks with water. Repeat with the remaining wheat and meat mixture and the filling until all are used up.

8 Heat the oil in a deep-fat fryer to 190°C (375°F). Deep-fry the kibbeh in batches for about 5 minutes until golden brown on all sides. Drain on absorbent kitchen paper. Serve hot or cold, with lemon for squeezing.

Menu Suggestion

In the Middle East, Kibbeh are traditionally served with a salad. A typical Arabic salad for serving with Kibbeh consists of radishes, green pepper, tomatoes and raw onion. Toss the salad in a dressing made with 60 ml (4 tbsp) tahini paste, the juice of 1 lemon, 150 ml (¼ pint) water, 45 ml (3 tbsp) olive oil and garlic, mint and salt and pepper to taste.

BIGOS
(POLISH CABBAGE AND MEAT)

| 2.00 | 🍳 | £ £ | ✳ | 270–405 cals |

Serves 4–6

225 g (8 oz) boneless leg or shoulder of pork

plain flour, for dredging

100 g (4 oz) Polish ham, smoked or salt

50 g (2 oz) flat mushrooms

450 g (1 lb) home-made sauerkraut (page 154), or bottled or canned sauerkraut

1 bay leaf

450 g (1 lb) firm cabbage heart, shredded

100 g (4 oz) streaky bacon rashers, rinded

1 large onion, skinned and chopped

50 g (2 oz) Polish sausage, skinned and diced

30 ml (2 tbsp) tomato purée

150 ml (¼ pint) red wine

1 garlic clove, skinned and crushed

salt and freshly ground pepper

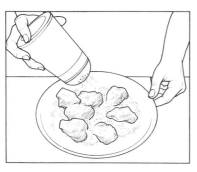

1 Cut the pork into 5 cm (2 inch) pieces and dredge with flour. Cut the ham and mushrooms into neat, even-sized strips.

2 Drain the sauerkraut, then put into a large pan with the bay leaf and 300 ml (½ pint) water. Bring to the boil and simmer for 30 minutes.

3 Meanwhile, put the cabbage and mushrooms into a separate pan, with 300 ml (½ pint) water. Bring to the boil then simmer for 30 minutes. Drain well.

4 With kitchen scissors, snip the bacon into a heavy-based frying pan. Fry in its own fat, then add to the sauerkraut.

5 Add the onion to the bacon fat and fry gently for about 10 minutes until golden. Add to the sauerkraut. Add more fat to the pan if necessary, then add the pork and fry until golden. Add the pork to the sauerkraut and simmer for about 1 hour, or until the pork is quite tender.

6 About 30 minutes before the dish is to be served, add the cabbage and mushrooms to the sauerkraut with the ham, sausage, tomato purée, wine, garlic, salt and pepper to taste. Bigos should be just juicy, not swimming in liquid. If necessary, a little extra boiling water can be added during cooking.

Menu Suggestion
In Poland, Bigos is traditionally served with rye bread or floury boiled potatoes. If you find rye bread too strong in flavour, serve Bigos with wholemeal or granary bread instead.

SHASHLIK
(CAUCASIAN LAMB KEBABS)

0.45*	✳*	723 cals

* plus at least 8 hours marinating;
freeze the lamb in the marinade

Serves 4

700–900 g (1½–2 lb) boneless lamb
  (eg fillet or leg), trimmed of fat

75 ml (5 tbsp) red wine vinegar

90 ml (6 tbsp) olive oil

10 ml (2 tsp) grated nutmeg

10 ml (2 tsp) dried marjoram

salt and freshly ground pepper

8 thick rashers of unsmoked fatty
  streaky bacon

4 small onions, skinned

16 bay leaves

extra olive oil, for brushing
  (if necessary)

1 Cut the lamb into large cubes
(if you cut the cubes too small
the lamb will cook too quickly and
not be juicy).

2 Put the wine vinegar, oil,
nutmeg and marjoram in a
bowl with plenty of pepper. Whisk
with a fork until well combined,
then add the cubes of lamb and
stir to coat in the marinade.

3 Cover the bowl and marinate
the lamb in the refrigerator for
at least 8 hours, turning
occasionally during this time.

4 When ready to cook, cut each
bacon rasher into 4–6 pieces,
discarding the rind and any small
pieces of bone.

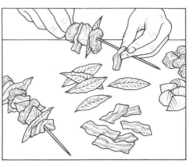

5 Cut the onions into eighths.
Thread the lamb, bacon,
onions and bay leaves on to 8 oiled
kebab skewers. Alternate the
ingredients as evenly as possible—
divide the meat equally between
the skewers, allow 4–6 pieces of
bacon per skewer, 4 onion pieces
and 2 bay leaves.

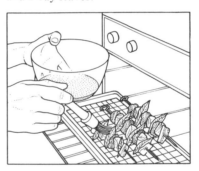

6 Cook over a charcoal barbecue
or under a preheated grill for
about 15 minutes until the lamb is
tender but still pink and juicy on
the inside. Turn the skewers
frequently during cooking and
baste with any remaining
marinade or olive oil. Sprinkle
with salt and pepper to taste
before serving.

Menu Suggestion
Serve Shashlik for a summer
barbecue meal in the garden.
Warm through pitta bread on the
barbecue grid for a few moments
and stuff the kebabs in the pockets
of bread. Accompany with lemon
wedges, a green salad and a tomato
and onion salad. Alternatively,
serve on a bed of rice.

CHINESE RED-COOKED PORK

2.30	£	887–1330 cals

Serves 4–6

1.8 kg (4 lb) rolled neck cnd of pork with skin
450 ml (¾ pint) chicken stock or water
200 ml (⅓ pint) soy sauce
4 garlic cloves, skinned and sliced
5 cm (2 inch) piece of fresh root ginger, peeled and sliced
10 ml (2 tsp) Chinese five-spice powder (see box)
60 ml (4 tbsp) sugar
150 ml (¼ pint) dry sherry

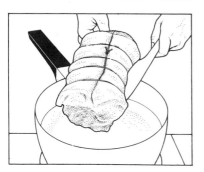

1 Bring a large saucepan of water to the boil. Add the pork and remove immediately, to scald it. Drain and pat dry.

2 Pour the stock into a large flameproof casserole. Add the soy sauce, garlic, ginger, five-spice powder and sugar. Bring to the boil, then lower the heat and simmer for 5 minutes.

3 Add the pork, skin side down, to the casserole and baste well. Cover and cook in the oven at 180°C (350°F) mark 4 for 1½ hours.

4 Remove the lid of the casserole, turn the meat skin side up and baste well with the juices. Return to the oven, uncovered, for another 30 minutes or until the pork is very tender, basting regularly.

5 Transfer the casserole to the top of the cooker. Add the dry sherry and then bring the juices to the boil.

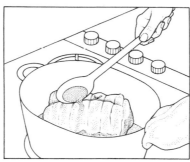

6 Boil rapidly for about 15 minutes, continually basting the meat until glazed. Take care that the meat does not catch or burn. Serve the meat sliced, hot or cold, with any remaining sauce.

Menu Suggestion
Red-Cooked Pork is rich and spicy. Serve with a contrasting plain accompaniment such as boiled rice, and follow with stir-fried crisp spring vegetables.

SWEET AND SOUR PORK

0.30	£	447 cals

Serves 4

700 g (1½ lb) boneless leg or shoulder of pork
20 ml (4 tsp) cornflour
salt and freshly ground pepper
vegetable oil for deep-frying, plus 15 ml (1 tbsp)
1 green pepper, cored, seeded and thinly sliced
30 ml (2 tbsp) sugar
30 ml (2 tbsp) white wine vinegar
30 ml (2 tbsp) tomato purée
30 ml (2 tbsp) pineapple juice
30 ml (2 tbsp) soy sauce
2 fresh or canned pineapple rings, finely chopped

1 Trim the fat off the pork, then cut the meat into 2.5 cm (1 inch) cubes. Coat in the corn-flour, reserving 5 ml (1 tsp) for the sauce. Add salt to taste.

2 Heat the vegetable oil in a deep-fat fryer to 180°C (350°F). Add half of the pork and deep-fry for 8–9 minutes or until tender. Remove with a slotted spoon and drain on absorbent kitchen paper. Keep hot while frying the remaining pork.

3 Make the sauce. Heat the 15 ml (1 tbsp) vegetable oil in a wok or frying pan, add the green pepper and stir-fry for 1 minute. Stir in the remaining ingredients with the reserved cornflour. Stir-fry for 1–2 minutes.

4 Add the pork and stir-fry for 1 minute. Taste and adjust seasoning, then turn into a warmed serving bowl. Serve hot.

Menu Suggestion
For a Chinese-style meal, serve Sweet and Sour Pork with white rice. Boil the rice, drain, then toss in a little sesame oil for an authentic flavour. Follow with a salad of raw beansprouts, grated carrot, shredded Chinese leaves and strips of cucumber. Toss the salad in an oil and vinegar dressing flavoured with soy sauce.

CHINESE RED-COOKED PORK
Five-spice powder is so called because it is a mixture of five different spices. Cinnamon, cloves, fennel, star anise and Szechuan peppercorns is the usual combination, but the blend can vary from one brand to another, so that not all five-spice powder tastes the same. Look for it in packets and small jars in Chinese specialist shops, and in some large supermarkets and delicatessens. It is not absolutely essential for this dish if you are unable to obtain it, ground mixed spice can be used instead.

SAG GOSHT
(INDIAN LAMB AND SPINACH CURRY)

2.00	✳	589 cals

Serves 4

1–2 garlic cloves, skinned and roughly chopped

2.5 cm (1 inch) piece of fresh root ginger, peeled and roughly chopped

15 ml (1 tbsp) mustard seeds

15 ml (1 tbsp) coriander seeds

5 ml (1 tsp) turmeric

2.5 ml ($\frac{1}{2}$ tsp) chilli powder or to taste

salt

65 g (2$\frac{1}{2}$ oz) ghee or butter

3 medium onions, skinned and thinly sliced

900 g (2 lb) boneless lamb fillet, trimmed of fat and cut into cubes

300 ml ($\frac{1}{2}$ pint) natural yogurt

450 g (1 lb) fresh spinach, trimmed and washed, or 225 g (8 oz) frozen leaf spinach, thawed

1 Put the garlic and ginger in a mortar and pestle with the mustard seeds and coriander. Pound until well crushed, then mix in the turmeric, chilli powder and 5 ml (1 tsp) salt.

2 Melt 50 g (2 oz) of the ghee in a flameproof casserole, add two-thirds of the onions and fry gently for about 10 minutes until softened and lightly coloured.

3 Add the crushed spice mixture and fry gently, stirring, for a few minutes. Add the lamb in batches, increase the heat and fry until well browned on all sides.

4 Return all the lamb to the casserole. Add the yogurt to the meat, 15 ml (1 tbsp) at a time. Stir-fry after each addition to mix with the meat, then cover and cook gently for 1 hour or until the lamb is tender.

5 Add the spinach to the casserole, stir well to mix with the meat and continue cooking for a further 5 minutes.

6 Meanwhile, melt the remaining ghee in a small frying pan, add the remaining sliced onion and fry, stirring constantly, over moderate heat until the onion is softened and golden.

7 Taste the curry and add more salt, if necessary. Turn into a warmed serving dish and sprinkle the golden onion slices over the top. Serve hot.

Menu Suggestion
The rich combination of spinach and lamb needs a plain accompaniment. Serve with boiled basmati rice, a yogurt and cucumber or onion raita, crispy poppadoms and chutneys.

RAAN
(INDIAN SPICED LAMB)

4.00*	£ £	685 cals

* plus 2–3 days marinating and 1 hour coming to room temperature

Serves 6

1.8 kg (4 lb) leg of lamb, skin and H-bone removed

6 large garlic cloves, skinned and roughly chopped

1 large piece of fresh root ginger, weighing about 50 g (2 oz), peeled and roughly chopped

300 ml ($\frac{1}{2}$ pint) natural yogurt

thinly pared rind and juice of 1 lemon

15 ml (1 tbsp) cumin seeds

seeds of 6 cardamom pods

6 whole cloves

150 g (5 oz) blanched almonds

10 ml (2 tsp) salt

5 ml (1 tsp) turmeric

5–10 ml (1–2 tsp) chilli powder, according to taste

1 Make deep slashes all over the leg of lamb with a sharp, pointed knife. Set aside while making the marinade.

2 Put the garlic and ginger in a blender or food processor with 60 ml (4 tbsp) of the yogurt, the lemon rind and juice, the cumin seeds, cardamom pods and cloves. Work to a paste.

3 Roughly chop 100 g (4 oz) of the almonds, then add to the machine with a few more spoonfuls of yogurt. Work again, then add the remaining yogurt with the salt, turmeric and chilli powder. Work until all the ingredients are thoroughly combined.

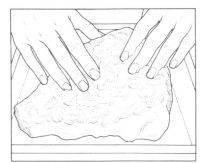

4 Put the leg of lamb in a roasting tin and spread all over with the spiced yogurt paste. Work the paste into the cuts in the meat as much as possible. Cover the lamb loosely with foil and marinate in the refrigerator for 2–3 days.

5 When ready to cook, uncover the lamb and allow the meat to come to room temperature for about 1 hour. Roast in the oven at 220°C (425°F) mark 7 for 30 minutes.

6 Lower the oven temperature to 180°C (350°F) mark 4 and roast for a further 1 hour, then lower the temperature to 170°C (325°F) mark 3 and roast for a further 2 hours, or until the meat is very tender and almost falling off the bone.

7 Remove the lamb from the roasting tin and place on a warmed serving platter. Cover loosely with foil and keep warm in a low oven.

8 Pour off the excess fat from the roasting tin, then place the tin on top of the cooker. Boil the sediment and juices to reduce, stirring and scraping the pan with a wooden spoon.

9 Uncover the lamb and pour over the pan juices. Arrange the remaining almonds over the lamb in a decorative 'flower' pattern. Serve hot.

Menu Suggestion
Raan is quite a spectacular dish to serve, either for a dinner party or for a special Sunday roast. Saffron rice looks good as an accompaniment, and *sag bhaji* (curried spinach) complements the flavour of the lamb well. Alternatively, serve with *sag aloo* (spinach and potato curry) instead of separate dishes of rice and spinach.

85

COLONIAL GOOSE

3.00*	🍴 🍴 £ £	620–827 cals

* plus 6 hours or overnight marinating
Serves 6–8

100 g (4 oz) dried apricots
1 small and 1 large onion, skinned
100 g (4 oz) fresh breadcrumbs
1.25 ml ($\frac{1}{4}$ tsp) dried thyme
25 g (1 oz) butter
15 ml (1 tbsp) clear honey
salt and freshly ground pepper
1 egg, beaten
2 kg (4$\frac{1}{2}$ lb) leg of lamb, boned
     (page 136)
225 g (8 oz) old carrots, peeled
150 ml ($\frac{1}{4}$ pint) red wine
1 bay leaf
3 parsley stalks, crushed
15 ml (1 tbsp) plain flour

1 Using scissors, snip the apricots into a bowl. Chop the small onion very finely and add to the apricots with the breadcrumbs and thyme.

2 Put the butter and honey in a small saucepan and heat gently until melted. Pour into the apricot mixture and add salt and pepper to taste. Add the beaten egg and bind together.

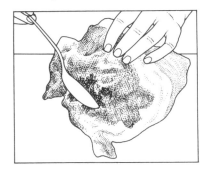

3 Place the meat, fat side down, on a wooden board and spoon the stuffing into the cavity from where the bone was removed. Push the stuffing well down into the leg with the back of the spoon.

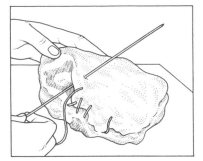

4 Sew up the lamb using string and a trussing needle. To prevent the skin from splitting during roasting, do not truss the joint too tightly.

5 Put the lamb into a large, heavy-guage polythene bag. Slice the large onion and the carrots and add to the bag with the wine, bay leaf and parsley. Leave in a cool place to marinate for about 6 hours or overnight, turning the meat occasionally in the marinade juices.

6 Remove the joint from the bag, strain the marinade and reserve. Weigh the joint and calculate the cooking time, allowing 25 minutes per 450 g (1 lb).

7 Place the joint on a rack standing over a roasting tin. Roast in the oven at 180°C (350°F) mark 4 for the calculated cooking time, basting occasionally. Transfer the joint to a warmed serving dish and keep hot in the oven turned to its lowest setting.

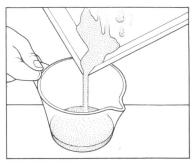

8 Pour off all but 30 ml (2 tbsp) of the fat from the roasting tin. Place the tin on top of the cooker and sprinkle in the flour. Blend well with a wooden spoon, then cook for 2–3 minutes, stirring continuously until golden brown.

9 Gradually stir in the reserved marinade and 300 ml ($\frac{1}{2}$ pint) water. Bring to the boil. Simmer for 2–3 minutes, then add salt and pepper to taste. Pour into a gravy boat or jug. Remove the string from the lamb and serve hot, with the gravy handed separately.

Menu Suggestion
Serve this traditional New Zealand dish for Sunday lunch, with roast potatoes, roast parsnips and seasonal vegetables.

COLONIAL GOOSE

Colonial Goose comes from New Zealand. Not surprisingly, it was originally a recipe for stuffed goose rather than lamb, but now that goose is expensive and New Zealand lamb so prolific, the stuffing has become a classic for lamb. There is also another version called 'One-Legged Goose', in which sage is used rather than the thyme, as here.

This recipe has a classic stuffing, but you can ring the changes with other ingredients from time to time. Boiled long grain rice (white or brown) can be used instead of breadcrumbs, mushrooms can be added for extra flavour, and other dried fruit such as prunes, sultanas or raisins can be used instead of the apricots.

Everyday Dishes

Family suppers, evening meals, weekend lunches —these are the dishes that are the most difficult to make. They have to be cooked with monotonous regularity—time is of the essence—and economy is all important. All these restrictions tend to dampen inspiration, but in this chapter you will find lots of ideas for quick, tasty and economical meals. They will fire your imagination without stretching your purse.

CHINESE PORK BROTH

| 1.45 | £ | ✳ | 274–412 cals |

Serves 4–6

450 g (1 lb) lean belly of pork

225 g (8 oz) carrots, peeled

4 spring onions, trimmed

30 ml (2 tbsp) vegetable oil

2.5 cm (1 inch) piece of fresh root ginger, peeled and cut into slivers

2.3 litres (4 pints) chicken stock

15 ml (1 tbsp) medium dry sherry

1 large garlic clove, skinned and crushed

125 g (4 oz) chick peas, soaked overnight then drained

salt and freshly ground pepper

450 g (1 lb) Chinese leaves, finely shredded

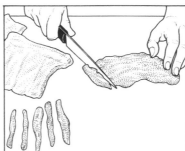

1 Cut the belly pork into fine strips, discarding the skin and bone. Slice the carrots into thin strips and cut the spring onions into 1 cm ($\frac{1}{2}$ inch) lengths.

2 Heat the oil in a wok or large saucepan, add the pork, carrots, onions and ginger and fry for about 6 minutes or until all the ingredients are browned.

3 Add the stock, sherry, garlic and chick peas, with pepper to taste. Bring to the boil, cover and simmer for about 1$\frac{1}{4}$ hours, or until the pork and chick peas are just tender. Skim if necessary.

4 Stir the Chinese leaves into the soup with salt to taste. Simmer for a further 5 minutes. Taste and adjust seasoning. Serve hot.

Menu Suggestion
Chinese Pork Broth is a substantial soup. For an everyday supper, serve with crisply fried prawn crackers, or Spring Rolls (page 29).

CHINESE PORK BROTH

Although some of the ingredients for this broth may sound exotic, they are all available at supermarkets and greengrocers. Chinese leaves are sometimes also called Chinese or Peking Cabbage, or even Chinese Celery Cabbage. They are used extensively in oriental cooking, and look like a cross between celery and large white Cos lettuce. The flavour of Chinese leaves is mildly bitter, but it is the crunchy texture that makes this vegetable so popular. It can be eaten raw in salads as a substitute for lettuce, especially in winter when most varieties of lettuce are so limp, and it is especially good in stir-fried dishes and soups. Do not confuse Chinese leaves with *bok choi*, sometimes described as Chinese greens. This vegetable looks similar, but it has dark green leaves and tastes more like Swiss chard or spinach. It can be used in this recipe if wished.

LENTIL, BACON AND VEGETABLE SOUP

| 2.15 | £ | 119–178 cals |

Serves 4–6

30 ml (2 tbsp) vegetable oil

15 g ($\frac{1}{2}$ oz) butter or margarine

1 large onion, skinned and roughly chopped

3 celery sticks, trimmed and roughly chopped

3 medium carrots, peeled and thinly sliced

75 g (3 oz) red lentils

1 bacon knuckle

10 ml (2 tsp) ground ginger

2.5 ml ($\frac{1}{2}$ tsp) ground cloves

salt and freshly ground pepper

chopped fresh parsley, to garnish

1 Heat the oil and butter in a large saucepan, add the onion, celery and carrots and fry gently, stirring, for 10 minutes until lightly coloured.

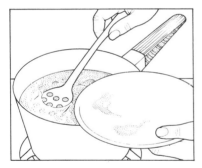

2 Add the lentils and 1.4 litres (2$\frac{1}{2}$ pints) water, then the bacon knuckle. Bring slowly to the boil and skim off any scum with a slotted spoon. Lower the heat, add the ginger, cloves and salt and pepper to taste, then half cover the pan and simmer for 1$\frac{1}{2}$ hours. Stir often, adding water if necessary.

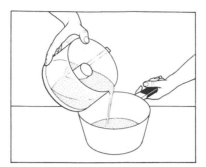

3 Remove the knuckle from the pan and set aside to cool slightly. Work the vegetables and liquid to a purée in a blender or food processor, then return to the rinsed–out pan. Reheat, stirring, then taste and adjust seasoning. Thin to the required consistency with water, if necessary.

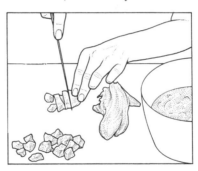

4 Strip the meat from the bacon knuckle and cut into bite-sized pieces. Add to the pan and heat through. Serve very hot, sprinkled with chopped parsley.

Menu Suggestion

This soup is thick and nourishing, just the food for an evening meal on a cold winter's day. Serve with crusty French bread or granary rolls and cheese, or with hot garlic or herb bread.

BARBECUED SPARERIBS

| 2.00 | £ | 392 cals |

Serves 4

about 1.8 kg (4 lb) Chinese-style
   pork spareribs
salt and freshly ground pepper
100 ml (4 fl oz) clear honey
60 ml (4 tbsp) dark soft brown
   sugar
60 ml (4 tbsp) tomato ketchup
30 ml (2 tbsp) Worcestershire sauce
30 ml (2 tbsp) French mustard
30 ml (2 tbsp) wine vinegar

1 If the butcher has not already
done so, cut the sheets of
spareribs into individual chops.

2 Place the ribs in 2 oiled
roasting tins and sprinkle with
salt and pepper. Roast the ribs in
the oven at 220°C (425°F) mark 7
for 20 minutes.

3 Meanwhile, put the remaining
ingredients in a jug and stir
well until mixed together.

4 Remove the ribs from the oven
and lower the temperature to
200°C (400°F) mark 6. Pour the
sauce into the tins and turn the
ribs until coated. Return to the
oven and roast for 1 hour. Turn
the ribs in the sauce several times
during cooking and swap over the
shelf positions of the 2 tins, if
necessary.

5 Lower the oven temperature
to 180°C (350°F) mark 4.
Turn the ribs over in the sauce
once more and continue roasting
for a further 30 minutes, or until
the meat is tender and the sauce
syrupy. Serve hot, with the sauce
poured over the ribs.

Menu Suggestion
Chinese-style spareribs should be
eaten with the fingers. They are
often served as a starter, but the
quantity here is plenty for a main
meal. Provide finger bowls and
plenty of paper napkins, for easy
eating. Boiled or fried rice and a
dish of stir-fried vegetables would
make good accompaniments.

BARBECUED SPARERIBS

Many supermarkets now sell
Chinese-style spareribs which
are ready-cooked and only have
to be reheated for serving. These
ribs are tasty but very expensive,
and yet raw from the butcher,
spareribs are one of the most
economical cuts of meat you can
buy. Not all butchers display
spareribs because they are so
bulky, but they are well worth

asking for. Do not confuse them
with sparerib chops, which are
thicker and meatier and from the
neck end of the animal. Chinese-
style spareribs are cut from the
thick end of the belly and are
sold in sheets. The butcher will
divide them into individual ribs
if requested, which makes them
easier to deal with.

CHILLI PORK AND BEANS

3.30*	£	465–698 cals

* plus overnight soaking

Serves 4–6

30 ml (2 tbsp) vegetable oil

900 g (2 lb) boneless pork shoulder, trimmed of fat and cut into cubes

1 large onion, skinned and roughly chopped

2 celery sticks, trimmed and sliced

1–2 garlic cloves, skinned and crushed

175 g (6 oz) red kidney beans, soaked in cold water overnight

15 ml (1 tbsp) black treacle

15 ml (1 tbsp) French mustard

5 ml (1 tsp) chilli powder

salt and freshly ground pepper

1 Heat 15 ml (1 tbsp) of the oil in a flameproof casserole, add the pork in batches and fry over high heat until coloured on all sides. Remove with a slotted spoon and drain on absorbent kitchen paper.

2 Lower the heat, then add the remaining oil to the pan with the onion, celery and garlic. Fry gently for 10 minutes until softened.

3 Drain the kidney beans and add to the pan with 1.1 litres (2 pints) water. Bring to the boil, stirring, then boil rapidly for 10 minutes to destroy any toxins in the beans.

4 Lower the heat, return the pork to the pan and add the black treacle, mustard, chilli powder and pepper to taste. Stir well to mix.

5 Cover the casserole and cook in the oven at 150°C (300°F) mark 2 for 3 hours. Stir the pork and beans occasionally during the cooking time and add more water if dry. Add 5 ml (1 tsp) salt half-way through, then taste and adjust seasoning before serving, adding more chilli powder if a hotter flavour is liked.

Menu Suggestion
Serve this hot Mexican-style dish for a family supper, with plain boiled rice and a salad of sliced avocado and tomato dressed with oil and lemon juice. A bowl of natural yogurt can also be served, to cool and refresh the palate.

PORK PAPRIKASH

| 2.30 | £ ✳* | 653 cals |

* freeze at the end of step 3

Serves 4

50 g (2 oz) butter or margarine

30 ml (2 tbsp) olive oil

900 g (2 lb) boneless pork sparerib, trimmed of excess fat and cut into cubes

450 g (1 lb) Spanish onions, skinned and thinly sliced

2 garlic cloves, skinned and crushed (optional)

15 ml (1 tbsp) paprika

10 ml (2 tsp) caraway seeds

450 ml ($\frac{3}{4}$ pint) chicken stock

salt and freshly ground pepper

about 150 ml ($\frac{1}{4}$ pint) soured cream and snipped chives, to finish

1 Heat half of the butter with the oil in a flameproof casserole, add the cubes of pork and fry over high heat for about 5 minutes until coloured on all sides. Remove with a slotted spoon to a plate.

2 Reduce the heat to very low and melt the remaining butter in the pan. Add the onions and garlic, if using, and fry very gently for about 30 minutes until very soft and golden, stirring frequently to prevent catching and burning.

3 Stir the paprika and caraway seeds into the onions, then add the pork and juices and mix well. Pour in the stock, add salt and pepper to taste and bring slowly to the boil, stirring. Cover and cook gently for about 1$\frac{1}{2}$ hours until the pork is tender.

4 Before serving, taste and adjust seasoning. Drizzle over soured cream and sprinkle with chives. Serve hot.

Menu Suggestion

Pork Paprikash is best served on a bed of noodles or rice. Accompany with a green vegetable such as broccoli, courgettes or French beans, or follow with a colourful mixed salad of shredded lettuce or endive, red and green pepper rings and sliced cucumber.

HUNTINGDON FIDGET PIE

1.15*	£	686 cals

* plus 30 minutes chilling

Serves 4

250 g (9 oz) plain flour

100 g (4 oz) butter or margarine

salt and freshly ground pepper

225 g (8 oz) streaky bacon, rinded
  and roughly chopped

1 medium onion, skinned and
  roughly chopped

225 g (8 oz) cooking apples, peeled,
  cored and roughly chopped

15 ml (1 tbsp) chopped parsley

150 ml ($\frac{1}{4}$ pint) medium cider

beaten egg, to glaze

1 Make the pastry. Sift 225 g (8 oz) of the flour and a pinch of salt into a bowl. Cut the butter into small pieces and rub into the flour until the mixture resembles breadcrumbs. Add enough water to mix to a firm dough.

2 Gather the dough into a ball and knead lightly. Wrap in foil and chill for 30 minutes.

3 Meanwhile, combine the bacon, onion and apples in a 600 ml (1 pint) pie dish. Add the parsley and salt and pepper.

4 Blend the remaining flour with the cider, a little at a time, and pour into the pie dish.

5 Roll out the pastry. Cut out a thin strip long enough to go around the rim of the pie dish. Moisten the rim with water and place the pastry strip on the rim.

6 Roll out the remaining pastry for a lid, moisten the strip of pastry, then place the lid on top and press to seal. Knock up and flute the edge.

7 Make a diagonal cross in the centre almost to the edges of the dish, then fold back to reveal the filling.

8 Brush the pastry with the beaten egg. Bake in the oven at 190°C (375°F) mark 5 for about 45 minutes, or until the pastry is golden and the filling is cooked.

Menu Suggestion
Serve with seasonal vegetables for an economical, yet tasty family supper. Tankards of beer, lager or cider make ideal drinks.

HUNTINGDON FIDGET PIE
Fidget or Fitchett Pie was traditionally made at harvest time to feed the hungry workers. Potatoes can be added to the filling.

FRUITY STUFFED PORK CHOPS

| 1.50 | 🥘 £ £ | 530 cals |

Serves 4

4 thick pork loin chops
60 ml (4 tbsp) vegetable oil
1 small onion, skinned and finely chopped
2 celery sticks, trimmed and finely chopped
25 g (1 oz) Italian risotto rice
450 ml ($\frac{3}{4}$ pint) chicken stock
finely grated rind and juice of 1 large orange
50 g (2 oz) 'no-need-to-soak' prunes
50 g (2 oz) dried apricots
50 g (2 oz) blanched almonds
5 ml (1 tsp) ground cinnamon
salt and freshly ground pepper

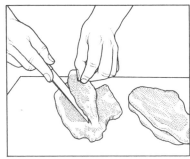

1 Using a sharp, pointed knife, make a horizontal cut in each pork chop, working from the outside fat edge to the bone. Trim off excess fat.

2 Make the stuffing. Heat 30 ml (2 tbsp) of the oil in a heavy-based saucepan, add the onion and celery and fry gently for 5 minutes until soft and lightly coloured.

3 Add the rice and stir well, then add 150 ml ($\frac{1}{4}$ pint) of the stock and half of the orange juice. Bring to the boil, stirring all the time. Lower the heat and simmer for 15–20 minutes, stirring frequently to prevent sticking and adding more stock if necessary. When the rice is cooked, turn into a bowl and leave to cool.

4 Meanwhile, stone the prunes and chop the flesh finely with the apricots and almonds. Add to the rice mixture with the cinnamon and salt and pepper to taste.

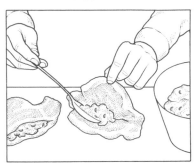

5 Spoon the stuffing into the cavities in the chops, then secure the open edges with wooden cocktail sticks. Reserve any remaining stuffing.

6 Heat the remaining oil in a flameproof casserole, add the chops and fry over moderate heat until browned on both sides, turning once. Pour in the remaining stock and orange juice, add any reserved rice stuffing with salt and pepper to taste and bring to the boil. Lower the heat, cover and simmer, basting frequently, for about 40 minutes until the chops are tender when pierced with a skewer.

7 Transfer to a warmed serving dish, pour over the pan juices and sprinkle with the grated orange rind. Serve hot.

Menu Suggestion
The risotto and dried fruit stuffing in these pork chops is sweet and spicy. Serve with extra risotto rice, and a mixed salad tossed in a sharp vinaigrette dressing to offset the sweetness.

LAMB IN TOMATO SAUCE WITH HERB BREAD

| 2.40 | ✳* | 747 cals |

* freeze lamb in tomato sauce only, without French bread

Serves 4

30 ml (2 tbsp) vegetable oil

1 kg (2¼ lb) boned lean shoulder of lamb, trimmed of fat and cubed

1 medium onion, skinned and sliced

20 ml (4 tsp) plain flour

397 g (14 oz) and 227 g (8 oz) can tomatoes

30 ml (2 tbsp) tomato purée

pinch of granulated sugar

2.5 ml (½ tsp) dried rosemary

60 ml (4 tbsp) red wine (optional)

salt and freshly ground pepper

lamb or beef stock, if necessary

40 g (1½ oz) butter

15 ml (1 tbsp) snipped fresh chives

eight 1 cm (½ inch) slices of French bread

1 Heat the oil in a flameproof casserole, add the lamb and fry over high heat until browned on all sides. Remove from the casserole with a slotted spoon and set aside.

2 Add the onion to the pan and fry for 5 minutes until soft. Stir in the flour and cook for 1 minute. Add the tomatoes with their juice, the tomato purée, sugar, rosemary and wine, if using. Bring to the boil, stirring all the time.

3 Return the meat to the pan and add salt and pepper to taste. Add a little stock, if necessary, to cover the meat. Cover the casserole and cook in the oven at 170°C (325°F) mark 3 for about 1¼ hours.

4 Meanwhile, make the herb butter. Beat the butter until smooth, then beat in the chives and salt and pepper to taste.

5 Spread the butter on to the slices of French bread. Uncover the casserole and place the bread, butter side up, on top. Cook for 1 further hour, or until the meat is tender. Serve hot.

Menu Suggestion

With its garnish of herb bread, this lamb casserole is quite a substantial dish. Serve simply, with a seasonal green vegetable.

LAMB IN TOMATO SAUCE WITH HERB BREAD

Shoulder of lamb is an excellent cut for casseroles such as this one, because it is so economical. It can be fatty, however, especially if the lamb is not an early-season, young animal. Check with your butcher before buying. An alternative cut of lamb which tends to be less fatty is the fillet. This cut comes from the middle neck and scrag; it is quite lean and tender, yet it does not become dry in casseroles as with the more expensive leg of lamb, which is too lean.

LAMB AND SPINACH LASAGNE

| 1.45 | 🍽 £ ✳* | 799 cals |

* freeze at the end of step 6

Serves 6

450 g (1 lb) fresh spinach, washed

30 ml (2 tbsp) vegetable oil

1 medium onion, skinned and chopped

450 g (1 lb) minced lamb

227 g (8 oz) can tomatoes

1 garlic clove, skinned and crushed

30 ml (2 tbsp) chopped fresh mint

5 ml (1 tsp) ground cinnamon

freshly grated nutmeg

salt and freshly ground pepper

50 g (2 oz) butter or margarine

50 g (2 oz) plain flour

900 ml ($1\frac{1}{2}$ pints) milk

150 ml ($\frac{1}{4}$ pint) natural yogurt

12–15 sheets oven-ready lasagne

175 g (6 oz) Feta or Cheddar cheese, grated

1 Put the spinach in a saucepan with only the water that clings to the leaves and cook gently for about 4 minutes. Drain well and chop finely.

2 Heat the oil in a large saucepan, add the onion and fry gently for 5 minutes until softened. Add the lamb and brown well, then drain off all the fat.

3 Stir in the spinach with the tomatoes and their juice, the garlic, mint and cinnamon. Season with nutmeg, salt and pepper to taste. Bring to the boil and simmer, uncovered, for about 30 minutes. Leave to cool while making the white sauce.

4 Melt the butter in a saucepan, add the flour and cook gently, stirring, for 1–2 minutes. Remove from the heat and gradually blend in the milk. Bring to the boil, stirring constantly, then simmer for 3 minutes until thick and smooth. Add the yogurt and salt and pepper to taste.

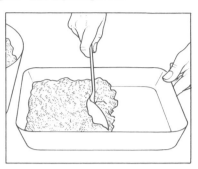

5 Spoon one-third of the meat mixture over the base of a rectangular baking dish.

6 Cover with 4–5 sheets of lasagne and spread over one-third of the white sauce. Repeat these layers twice more, finishing with the sauce, which should completely cover the lasagne. Sprinkle the cheese on top.

7 Stand the dish on a baking sheet. Bake in the oven at 180°C (350°F) mark 4 for 45–50 minutes, or until the top is well browned and bubbling. Serve hot.

Menu Suggestion

Lamb and Spinach Lasagne is rich and filling. Serve with a tomato salad dressed with oil, lemon juice and raw onion rings, chopped spring onion or snipped fresh chives.

SPICED LENTIL BAKE

2.30 £ 630 cals

Serves 4

45 ml (3 tbsp) vegetable oil

8 middle neck lamb chops, total
weight about 1.1 kg (2½ lb),
trimmed of excess fat

2 medium onions, skinned and
thinly sliced

15 ml (1 tbsp) turmeric

5 ml (1 tsp) paprika

5 ml (1 tsp) ground cinnamon

75 g (3 oz) red lentils

salt and freshly ground pepper

450 g (1 lb) potatoes, peeled and
thinly sliced

450 g (1 lb) swede, peeled and thinly
sliced

300 ml (½ pint) lamb or chicken
stock

1 Heat the oil in a large sauté
or frying pan, add the chops
and brown well on both sides.
Remove from the pan with a
slotted spoon.

2 Add the onions to the pan with
the turmeric, paprika,
cinnamon and lentils. Fry for 2–3
minutes. Add plenty of salt and
pepper and spoon into a shallow
2 litre (3½ pint) ovenproof dish.

3 Place the chops on top of the
onion and lentil mixture.
Arrange the vegetable slices on top
of the chops, then season and
pour over the stock.

4 Cover the dish tightly and
cook in the oven at 180°C
(350°F) mark 4 for about 1½
hours, or until the chops are
tender. Uncover and cook for a
further 30 minutes, or until lightly
browned on top. Serve hot,
straight from the dish.

Menu Suggestion

Spiced Lentil Bake is a complete
meal in itself, with lamb chops,
lentils, potatoes and swede baked
together in one dish. Serve with a
crisp green salad or a seasonal
green vegetable.

SPICED LENTIL BAKE

The different kinds of lentils
available can be confusing,
especially in health food shops
where there is always such a large
selection. The red lentils used in
this recipe are the most common
kind, sometimes also described
as 'split red lentils' or even
'Egyptian lentils'. They do not
need soaking and are quick-
cooking, but they tend to lose
their shape. 'Continental lentils'
are green, brown or reddish-
brown in colour, and are whole
rather than split. These varieties
keep their shape and have a
nuttier texture than red lentils,
but take longer to cook.

MARINATED LAMB WITH ONION PURÉE

| 0.55* | £ | ✳ | 560 cals |

* plus 1 hour marinating

Serves 4

45 ml (3 tbsp) olive oil

15 ml (1 tbsp) white wine vinegar

1.25 ml ($\frac{1}{4}$ tsp) dried sage

1 garlic clove, skinned and crushed

4 lamb chump chops, weighing about 225 g (8 oz) each

2 medium onions, skinned and finely chopped

30 ml (2 tbsp) plain flour

300 ml ($\frac{1}{2}$ pint) milk

1 clove

30 ml (2 tbsp) single cream

salt and freshly ground pepper

fresh sage sprigs, to garnish

1 In a jug, whisk together the olive oil, vinegar, sage and crushed garlic.

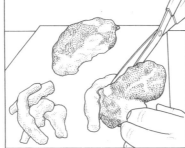

2 Trim the chops of any excess fat. Place the chops flat in a shallow glass or ceramic dish. Pour over the marinade, cover and leave to marinate in a cool place for 1 hour.

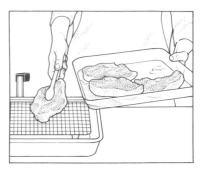

3 Remove the chops from the marinade and place under a preheated hot grill. Cook for 7–10 minutes on each side.

4 Meanwhile, put the marinade and chopped onions in a small saucepan. Cover and cook over low heat, for about 10–15 minutes until onions are soft and golden.

5 Stir in the flour, then the milk and clove. Bring to the boil and simmer for 2 minutes. Discard the clove, transfer to a blender or food processor and work until smooth. Return the sauce to the rinsed-out pan. Add the cream and salt and pepper to taste and reheat gently. Arrange the chops on a warmed serving dish and garnish with sprigs of sage. Serve the onion purée separately.

Menu Suggestion

These grilled chump chops are served with a tasty onion purée. Jacket baked potatoes topped with soured cream would make a delicious accompaniment for a warming meal in winter.

LIVER GOUJONS WITH ORANGE SAUCE

| 0.40 | £ | 607 cals |

Serves 4

350 g (12 oz) lamb's liver, sliced

75 ml (5 tbsp) plain flour

salt and freshly ground pepper

1 egg, beaten

125 g (4 oz) medium oatmeal

50 g (2 oz) butter or margarine

1 medium onion, sliced

300 ml ($\frac{1}{2}$ pint) lamb or beef stock

finely grated rind and juice of 1 medium orange

5 ml (1 tsp) dried sage

few drops of gravy browning

60 ml (4 tbsp) vegetable oil

1 Cut the liver into 5 cm (2 inch) pencil-thin strips. Coat evenly in 45 ml (3 tbsp) of the flour, liberally seasoned with salt and freshly ground pepper.

2 Dip the liver in the beaten egg, then roll in the oatmeal to coat. Chill in the refrigerator while preparing the sauce.

3 Melt 25 g (1 oz) of the butter in a saucepan, add the onion and fry gently until golden brown. Add the remaining flour and cook gently, stirring, for 1–2 minutes.

4 Gradually blend in the stock, orange rind and juice, sage and salt and pepper to taste. Bring to the boil, stirring constantly, then simmer for 10–15 minutes. Add the gravy browning and taste and adjust seasoning.

5 Heat the remaining butter and the oil in a frying pan, add the liver goujons and fry gently for 1–2 minutes until tender.

6 Arrange the goujons on a warmed serving platter and pour over a little of the sauce. Hand the remaining sauce separately in a sauceboat or jug.

Menu Suggestion

Serve on a bed of tagliatelle or Chinese noodles, and accompany with a green vegetable, or crunchy salad of raw beansprouts, celery and finely chopped walnuts, unsalted peanuts or cashews.

LIVER GOUJONS

The French word *goujon* is used in cooking to describe small strips or thin slivers of food; fish is often cut into goujons, then coated in egg and breadcrumbs before deep-frying. In this recipe, goujons of liver are coated in egg and oatmeal, which gives a nutty crunch to the coating, contrasting well with the soft texture of the liver inside. Orange is a popular flavour with liver in France, so too is vermouth. To give the dish an added 'kick', add a splash of dry vermouth with the orange juice in step 4.

LIVER AND BACON WITH POTATO PANCAKES

| 1.00 | ⏢ | £ | 662 cals |

Serves 4

2 large potatoes, peeled

1 egg, beaten

60 ml (4 tbsp) self raising flour

salt and freshly ground pepper

vegetable oil and butter (optional),
  for frying

450 g (1 lb) lamb's liver, cut thickly

25 g (1 oz) plain flour

8 rashers of back bacon

2 medium onions, skinned and
  finely sliced

10 ml (2 tsp) wine vinegar

30 ml (2 tbsp) chopped fresh
  parsley, to garnish

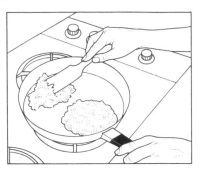

4 Cook the pancakes for about 5 minutes on each side until golden brown. Remove from the pan and drain on absorbent kitchen paper. Keep hot in the oven while cooking the liver.

5 Remove any ducts from the liver and discard. Dip the liver in the plain flour seasoned with salt and pepper. Heat a little oil or butter in a frying pan, add the liver and fry for 3–4 minutes on each side (it should still be slightly pink inside). Cover and keep hot.

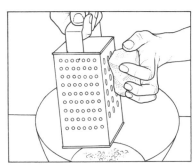

1 Grate the potatoes finely. Place in a sieve and rinse under cold water. Leave to drain for about 15 minutes. Wrap the potato in a clean tea towel and squeeze out any excess moisture.

2 Put the grated potatoes in a bowl. Add the egg, self raising flour and salt and pepper to taste, then mix well together.

3 Heat enough oil in a frying pan to come 0.5 cm (¼ inch) up the sides. When hot, add large spoonfuls of potato mixture, pressing them into flat pancakes with a spatula or fish slice.

6 Add the bacon to the pan and fry over brisk heat until crisp. Keep hot, but do not cover as it will become soggy.

7 Add the onions to the pan and cook for 5 minutes until just beginning to brown. Remove from the pan and arrange on a serving dish. Top with the liver and bacon and keep warm.

8 Add the vinegar and 45 ml (3 tbsp) water to the frying pan. Bring to the boil, scraping up any sediment from the bottom of the pan. Pour over the liver and bacon, then garnish with chopped parsley. Serve with the pancakes.

Menu Suggestion
This dish of fried liver, bacon and onions has its own accompaniment in the potato pancakes. Serve with colourful vegetables such as grilled tomatoes and peas.

SAUTÉED KIDNEYS WITH TOMATOES

| 0.50 | £ | ✳ | 444–592 cals |

Serves 3–4

12 lamb's kidneys
45 ml (3 tbsp) plain flour
25 g (1 oz) butter or margarine
30 ml (2 tbsp) vegetable oil
1 large onion, skinned and sliced
100 g (4 oz) mushrooms, sliced
397 g (14 oz) can tomatoes
15–20 ml (3–4 tsp) French mustard
salt and freshly ground pepper
chopped fresh parsley, to garnish

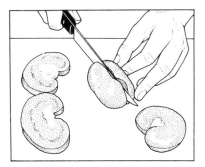

1 Wash the kidneys, cut them in half lengthways and, using scissors, remove the cores. Toss the kidneys in the flour.

2 Heat the butter and oil in a large flameproof casserole or frying pan, add the onion and fry for about 5 minutes until the onion is softened and golden brown.

3 Add the kidneys to the pan with any remaining flour and cook for 3–4 minutes, stirring occasionally, until lightly browned. Add the mushrooms and cook for a further 2–3 minutes.

4 Stir in the tomatoes with their juice, the mustard and salt and pepper to taste. Bring to the boil, stirring all the time, then cover and simmer for 5 minutes until tender. Serve hot, garnished with chopped parsley.

Menu Suggestion
Sautéed kidneys are light, but very tasty. Serve in a ring of brown rice, with chopped nuts, pimientos or peppers and sliced olives, if liked. Hot garlic bread would also make a good accompaniment, to help mop up the juices. Follow with a crisp and crunchy green salad, to refresh the palate.

SAUTÉED KIDNEYS WITH TOMATOES

It is well worth encouraging your family to eat kidneys. They are inexpensive to buy, yet extremely rich in iron, and in vitamins too. Take care not to exceed the cooking time given in the recipe. Overcooked kidneys are tough and rubbery.

SHEPHERD'S PIE

| 1.00 | £ | ✳ | 524 cals |

Serves 4

700 g (1½ lb) potatoes, peeled

salt and freshly ground pepper

450 g (1 lb) cooked lamb

30 ml (2 tbsp) vegetable oil

1 medium onion, skinned and chopped

30 ml (2 tbsp) plain flour

300 ml (½ pint) lamb or beef stock

15 ml (1 tbsp) Worcestershire sauce

90 ml (6 tbsp) chopped fresh parsley

5 ml (1 tsp) dried marjoram

50 g (2 oz) Cheddar cheese, grated

chopped fresh parsley, to garnish

1 Cook the potatoes in a saucepan of boiling salted water for about 20 minutes until tender.

2 Meanwhile, trim the excess fat from the lamb and discard. Chop finely or mince coarsely.

3 Heat the oil in a frying pan, add the onion and fry for about 5 minutes until lightly browned. Stir in the flour and fry for 2–3 minutes. Add the stock and simmer, stirring, until thickened.

4 Stir in the lamb, Worcestershire sauce, parsley, marjoram and salt and pepper. Spoon into a 1.1 litre (2 pint) shallow pie dish.

5 Drain the potatoes. Mash well, then gradually beat in the cheese and salt and pepper. Spoon or pipe over the lamb.

6 Bake in the oven at 200°C (400°F) mark 6 for 30 minutes until well browned. Serve hot, sprinkled with chopped parsley.

Menu Suggestion

Traditional vegetables to serve with Shepherd's Pie are cabbage or spring greens. To ensure that the nutrients are retained, shred the leaves, blanch and stir-fry rather than boiling.

SHEPHERD'S PIE

Although not traditional, Shepherd's Pie tastes extra good if you add mashed carrots or swedes to the potato topping. You can add as many or as few as you like, but a good proportion is half the weight of root vegetable to potato. Carrots and swedes not only add flavour, they also give the topping a warming golden-yellow colour.

Entertaining

Lamb and pork are both versatile meats for entertaining. Choose from such lean and tender cuts as joints, noisettes, chops, fillet and escalopes, or go for something completely different and cook sweetbreads for your guests. In this chapter, there is a wide choice of deliciously different dishes, to suit every special occasion imaginable.

LOIN OF PORK WITH FRUIT STUFFING

| 3.30 | 🗂 £ £ | 636 cals |

Serves 6

1.8 kg (4 lb) boned loin of pork

10 ml (2 tsp) ground allspice

salt and freshly ground pepper

4 garlic cloves, skinned

225 g (8 oz) mixed dried fruit (eg pears, prunes, apricots, figs)

100 g (4 oz) fresh cranberries or frozen cranberries, thawed

300 ml (½ pint) full-bodied red wine

2–3 bay leaves

30 ml (2 tbsp) bottled cranberry sauce

fresh bay leaves, to garnish

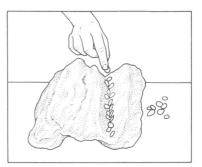

1 Cut the rind off the pork, together with all but a very thin layer of fat next to the meat.

2 Lay the meat flat, fat side down. Slice lengthways, two-thirds through the thick side of the 'eye' of the meat.

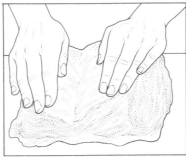

3 Open up the joint like a book. Rub the allspice into the flesh, with salt and pepper to taste.

4 Cut the garlic cloves into thin slivers, then place at regular intervals along the length of the meat. Chop the dried fruit finely, mix with the cranberries, then place on top of the garlic.

5 Form the joint into a roll and tie at close intervals. Weigh the joint and calculate the cooking time, allowing 35 minutes per 450 g (1 lb) plus 35 minutes. Put the joint in a large flameproof casserole or roasting tin and place over moderate heat. Fry the joint in its own fat until browned on all sides, then pour in the wine. Add the bay leaves and seasoning.

6 Bring to the boil, then cover and cook in the oven at 150°C (300°F) mark 2 for the calculated cooking time. Baste frequently and turn the joint round in the liquid every 30 minutes.

7 Place the joint on a warmed serving dish and leave to stand in a warm place for 15 minutes before carving. Transfer the casserole or tin to the top of the cooker. Discard the bay leaves, then boil the cooking liquid to reduce slightly. Stir in the cranberry sauce and heat through, then pour into a gravy boat or jug. Slice the pork and garnish with fresh bay leaves.

Menu Suggestion

Serve with sauté potatoes, broccoli and fennel.

LAMB NOISETTES WITH MUSHROOMS AND ONIONS

1.00–1.10 £ £ ✳

404–605 cals

Serves 4–6

12 noisettes of lamb (page 137)

plain flour, for coating

15 g (½ oz) butter

30 ml (2 tbsp) vegetable oil

225 g (8 oz) button onions, skinned

1 garlic clove, skinned and finely
  chopped

450 g (1 lb) small button
  mushrooms

300 ml (½ pint) dry white wine

sprig of fresh rosemary or 2.5 ml
  (½ tsp) dried

salt and freshly ground pepper

sprigs of fresh rosemary, to
  garnish

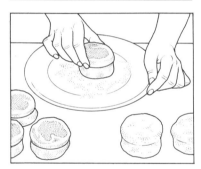

1 Coat the lamb in flour. Heat
the butter and oil in a large
frying pan or flameproof casserole,
add the noisettes and brown
quickly on both sides. Remove.

2 Add the onions and garlic and
fry for about 5 minutes until
lightly browned. Add the mushrooms and fry for 2–3 minutes.

3 Stir in the wine, rosemary and
salt and pepper to taste.
Replace the noisettes, bring to the
boil, then cover and simmer for
about 30–40 minutes until tender,
turning once.

4 Remove the string from the
noisettes and arrange on a
warmed serving dish. Add the
vegetables and keep warm.

5 Bring the remaining liquid to
the boil and boil rapidly until
reduced by half. Pour the wine
sauce over the noisettes and serve
garnished with sprigs of fresh
rosemary.

Menu Suggestion

Noisettes of lamb in a white wine
sauce are quick to make for an
informal supper party. Serve with
crisply cooked green vegetables
such as mange-touts, French
beans or broccoli, and a dish of
noodles tossed in melted butter
and a light sprinkling of poppy
seeds. Dry white wine would be
the appropriate drink to serve.

**LAMB NOISETTES WITH
MUSHROOMS AND
ONIONS**

To give this dish more of a
'French' flavour, add a splash of
an aniseed spirit such as Pernod
or Pastis to the sauce, at the same
time as adding the wine. In
France, the combination of lamb
and aniseed is very popular,
especially with the flavours of
garlic and rosemary. When
buying fresh garlic, look for the
type with purple skin. This is the
continental variety of garlic,
which has sweet, juicy flesh.

FILET DE PORC CHASSEUR
(FRENCH PORK FILLET IN WHITE WINE WITH MUSHROOMS)

| 2.30 | £ | ✳* | 696 cals |

* freeze after step 5

Serves 6

1 kg (2¼ lb) pork fillet or tenderloin

vegetable oil, for frying

65 g (2½ oz) butter

2 medium onions, skinned and
  chopped

225 g (8 oz) button mushrooms

45 ml (3 tbsp) plain flour

150 ml (¼ pint) beef stock

150 ml (¼ pint) dry white wine

salt and freshly ground pepper

twelve 1 cm (½ inch) slices of
  French bread

chopped fresh parsley, to garnish

1 Cut the pork fillet into 3–4 cm
(1¼–1½ inch) pieces. Heat 30 ml
(2 tbsp) of the oil in a frying pan,
add the pork and brown quickly.
Transfer to a casserole.

2 Melt 50 g (2 oz) of the butter
in the frying pan, add the
onion and fry for 5 minutes.

3 Add the mushrooms to the
pan, increase the heat and fry
for 1–2 minutes, tossing constantly. Remove with a slotted
spoon and place over the meat.

4 Blend the flour into the juices
in the pan, with the remaining
butter. Cook, stirring, for 1–2
minutes, then gradually blend in
the stock, wine and salt and
pepper. Simmer for 2–3 minutes.
Pour into the casserole.

5 Cover and cook in the oven at
170°C (325°F) mark 3 for
about 1¾ hours, or until the pork
is fork tender.

6 Meanwhile, heat oil in a frying
pan, add the French bread
slices and fry until golden brown
on each side. Drain well on
absorbent kitchen paper.

7 Serve the pork hot, sprinkled
liberally with chopped parsley
and garnished with French bread.

Menu Suggestion
Pork fillet cooked with white wine
and mushrooms is an excellent
main course for a dinner party.
The garnish of French bread slices
is an unusual serving idea, which
makes the dish quite substantial.
Suitable vegetable accompaniments would be mange-touts,
courgettes or French beans.

NORMANDY PORK

| 1.30 | 🍴 🍴 | £ £ | 688 cals |

Serves 4

8 thinly cut lean pork loin chops, trimmed of rind and excess fat

15 ml (1 tbsp) plain flour

salt and freshly ground pepper

50 g (2 oz) butter

30 ml (2 tbsp) olive oil

300 ml ($\frac{1}{2}$ pint) dry French cider

30 ml (2 tbsp) finely chopped fresh parsley

3 crisp eating apples

45 ml (3 tbsp) apple brandy or brandy

60 ml (4 tbsp) double cream

1 Coat the chops lightly in the flour seasoned with salt and pepper. Heat 25 g (1 oz) of the butter and 15 ml (1 tbsp) of the oil in a flameproof casserole, add the chops, a few at a time, and fry over moderate heat until browned on both sides.

2 Return all the chops to the pan and pour in the cider. Bring to the boil, then lower the heat and add the parsley. Cover and simmer gently for 30–40 minutes, or until the chops are tender.

3 Remove the chops from the pan and arrange, overlapping, on a warmed serving platter. Cover loosely with foil and keep hot in a low oven. Pour the cooking liquid into a jug.

4 Quarter and core the apples, but do not peel them. Slice the quarters thickly. Heat the remaining butter and the remaining oil in the casserole. Add the apple slices and toss over moderate heat for a few minutes until golden but still crisp.

5 Heat the brandy very gently in a small saucepan or ladle. Remove the casserole from the heat. Ignite the brandy, then pour flaming over the apple slices in the casserole.

6 Arrange the apple slices around the pork. Pour the cooking liquid back into the pan and reheat. Stir in the cream and heat through gently, then taste and adjust seasoning. Pour the sauce over the chops and serve immediately.

Menu Suggestion
Normandy Pork is a very rich and satisfying dinner party dish. Serve with plain accompaniments such as new potatoes cooked in their skins, and a chicory, endive or radicchio salad.

CIDER PORK SAUTÉ

1.45	536 cals

Serves 4

450 g (1 lb) green dessert apples

450 g (1 lb) floury old potatoes (eg King Edwards)

salt and freshly ground pepper

50 g (2 oz) butter

450 g (1 lb) pork escalope

15 ml (1 tbsp) vegetable oil

1 small onion, skinned and finely chopped

15 ml (1 tbsp) plain flour

300 ml ($\frac{1}{2}$ pint) dry cider

30 ml (2 tbsp) capers

beaten egg, to glaze

1 Peel half of the apples. Halve, core and slice thickly. Peel the potatoes, then cut them into small chunks.

2 Cook the prepared apples and potatoes together in a saucepan of salted water for 20 minutes or until the potatoes are tender. Drain well.

3 Press the apples and potatoes through a sieve into a bowl. Beat in 25 g (1 oz) of the butter, then add salt and pepper to taste.

4 Spoon or pipe the mixture down both ends of a 1.4 litre (2$\frac{1}{2}$ pint) shallow ovenproof dish.

5 Meanwhile, cut the pork escalope into fine strips. Quarter and core the remaining apples (but do not peel them). Slice them thickly into a bowl of cold water.

6 Heat the remaining butter and the oil in a large frying pan, add the pork strips, a few at a time, and fry until browned. Remove with a slotted spoon.

7 Add the onion to the pan and fry for 2–3 minutes. Return all the pork strips and stir in the flour. Cook, stirring, for 1–2 minutes, then blend in the cider and bring to the boil.

8 Drain the apple slices and stir into the pork. Simmer gently for 4–5 minutes, or until the pork is tender but the apple still holds its shape. Stir in the capers, with salt and pepper to taste.

9 Spoon the mixture into the centre of the dish. Brush the potato with beaten egg. Bake in the oven at 200°C (400°F) mark 6 for 25–30 minutes until golden. Serve hot, straight from the dish.

Menu Suggestion

Cider Pork Sauté is ideal for mid-week entertaining. Potatoes are included, so all you need is a seasonal vegetable like creamed spinach or a purée of sprouts.

MISHMISHIYA
(PERSIAN LAMB AND APRICOT STEW)

| 1.55* | £ £ ✳ | 782 cals |

* plus 2 hours soaking

Serves 4

225 g (8 oz) dried apricots

2.3 kg (5 lb) leg of lamb, boned and trimmed of fat

15 ml (1 tbsp) vegetable oil

1 large onion, skinned and chopped

5 ml (1 tsp) ground coriander

5 ml (1 tsp) ground cumin

2.5 ml ($\frac{1}{2}$ tsp) ground cinnamon

25 g (1 oz) ground almonds

salt and freshly ground pepper

1 Put the apricots in a bowl, cover with 300 ml ($\frac{1}{2}$ pint) boiling water and leave to soak for 2 hours. Cut the meat into 2.5 cm (1 inch) cubes.

2 Drain the apricots, reserving the liquid. Heat the oil in a large saucepan, add the lamb and onion and cook for 10 minutes, stirring, until lightly browned. Add the spices, almonds and salt and pepper to taste, then add the reserved apricot soaking liquid.

3 Cut the apricots in half and stir them into the lamb. Cover and simmer gently for 1$\frac{1}{2}$ hours, or until the lamb is tender, stirring occasionally. Serve hot.

Menu Suggestion
This Persian dish is rich and spicy. Serve with a nutty rice pilaf and okra (ladies' fingers) or courgettes tossed in grated lime rind, lime juice and chopped fresh coriander.

NOISETTES DE PORC TOURAINE
(FRENCH PORK NOISETTES WITH WINE, PRUNES AND CREAM)

1.00*	🍴	£ £	670 cals

* plus soaking time for the prunes

Serves 4

12–16 large, plump prunes

300 ml (½ pint) dry white wine

700 g (1½ lb) pork fillet or tenderloin

25 ml (1½ tbsp) plain flour

salt and freshly ground pepper

25 g (1 oz) butter

15 ml (1 tbsp) olive oil

30 ml (2 tbsp) port

15 ml (1 tbsp) redcurrant jelly

150 ml (¼ pint) double cream

1 Put the prunes in a bowl, pour in the wine, cover and leave to soak overnight, or according to packet instructions.

2 The next day, when ready to cook, lift the prunes out of the liquid with a slotted spoon and set aside. Reserve the soaking liquid.

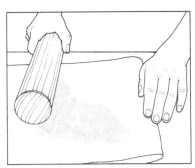

3 Cut the pork fillet into 0.5 cm (¼ inch) slices. Place the slices in a single layer between 2 sheets of greaseproof paper. Using a meat cleaver, mallet or rolling pin, bat the meat out thinly.

4 Coat the slices of pork in the flour seasoned with salt and pepper. Heat the butter and oil in a large, flameproof casserole, add as many pork slices as the pan will hold in a single layer and fry over moderate heat until golden brown on both sides. Remove and drain on absorbent kitchen paper while frying the remaining slices.

5 Pour the soaking liquid from the prunes into the casserole and stir to scrape up any sediment from the base and sides of the pan. Add the prunes and simmer for 20 minutes or until just tender, then return the pork to the pan and simmer for 8–10 minutes or until the meat is tender.

6 Arrange the pork slices overlapping on a warmed serving dish and surround with the prunes. Cover loosely with foil and keep hot in a low oven. Stir the port and redcurrant jelly into the cooking liquid and boil rapidly until reduced. Lower the heat, slowly stir in the cream and heat through gently. Taste and adjust seasoning, then drizzle over the pork. Serve immediately.

Menu Suggestion
Pork fillet with prunes, wine, port and cream is a sumptuously rich dinner party dish. Serve with the plainest of accompaniments such as new potatoes, and a green vegetable or a dressed salad. To be authentic, use a white Vouvray wine in the sauce, then serve the same wine to drink, well chilled.

LAMB CHOPS RATATOUILLE

1.00 £ £ ✱* 558 cals

* freeze the ratatouille only

Serves 4

1 small aubergine

salt and freshly ground pepper

45 ml (3 tbsp) olive oil

1 large onion, skinned and roughly
chopped

2 garlic cloves, skinned and
crushed

1 small red pepper, cored, seeded
and thinly sliced

1 small green pepper, cored,
seeded and thinly sliced

3 medium courgettes, trimmed
and sliced

450 g (1 lb) ripe tomatoes, skinned
and roughly chopped

150 ml (¼ pint) dry white wine

15 ml (1 tbsp) chopped fresh basil
or 7.5 ml (1½ tsp) dried basil

12 loin chops

50 g (2 oz) butter

1 Slice the aubergine thinly and place in a colander, sprinkling salt between each layer. Cover with a plate, place heavy weights on top, then leave to dégorge for 20 minutes.

2 Meanwhile, heat the oil in a large, heavy-based saucepan, add the onion and garlic and fry gently for about 5 minutes until soft and lightly coloured.

3 Add the peppers to the pan and fry gently for a few minutes, stirring, then stir in the courgettes. Rinse the aubergine slices under cold running water, then add to the pan with the tomatoes, wine, basil and salt and pepper to taste.

4 Stir well to mix and bring to the boil, then lower the heat, cover and simmer very gently for 30 minutes. At the end of cooking time the vegetables should be soft and juicy, stir frequently during cooking and add a few spoonfuls of water if there is not enough liquid in the pan.

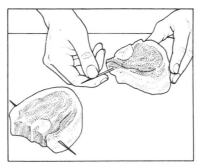

5 Meanwhile, trim as much fat as possible off the lamb chops. Curl the 'apron' around the eye of the meat and secure with wooden cocktail sticks.

6 Melt the butter in 1 or 2 heavy-based frying pans. Add the chops and fry over high heat until seared on both sides, then lower the heat and cook for a further 5 minutes on each side until the meat is tender, but still pink on the inside.

7 Taste and adjust the seasoning of the ratatouille, then transfer to a warmed serving dish. Arrange the chops on top and serve immediately.

Menu Suggestion

These lamb chops come with their own mixed vegetables, and are very quick to prepare and easy to serve — ideal for an informal mid-week dinner party. The French potato dish *gratin dauphinois*, rich with cream and Gruyère cheese, would complement the flavour of the lamb and vegetables, and could be prepared the night before.

SWEETBREADS WITH MUSHROOMS AND WHITE WINE

| 1.00* | 🗋 | £ £ | 520 cals |

* plus 4 hours soaking

Serves 4

700 g (1½ lb) lamb's sweetbreads, thawed if frozen

salt and freshly ground pepper

1 onion, skinned and chopped

1 carrot, peeled and sliced

1 celery stick

1 bouquet garni

300 ml (½ pint) dry white wine

25 g (1 oz) butter

15 ml (1 tbsp) olive oil

225 g (8 oz) button mushrooms, halved or sliced if large

150 ml (¼ pint) double cream

20 ml (4 tsp) chopped fresh basil or 5 ml (1 tsp) dried

fresh basil sprigs, to garnish

1 Soak the sweetbreads in salted water for about 4 hours to remove traces of blood. Change the water frequently until the sweetbreads turn white. Drain and rinse under cold running water.

2 Plunge the sweetbreads into a pan of boiling salted water and blanch for 2–3 minutes. Drain and set aside to cool.

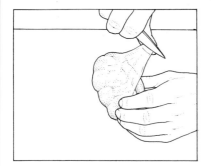

3 Peel off the skin from the sweetbreads with your fingers, then cut away all gristle and stringy tissue. Slice the sweetbreads thinly.

4 Put the sweetbreads in a saucepan with the onion, carrot, celery and bouquet garni. Pour in the wine and add salt and pepper to taste.

5 Bring to the boil, then lower the heat, cover and simmer for 10 minutes, or until the sweetbreads feel tender when pierced with a skewer. Remove the sweetbreads from the pan with a slotted spoon, discard the vegetables and boil the cooking liquid to reduce to 150 ml (¼ pint).

6 Heat the butter and oil in a heavy-based frying pan, add the mushrooms and fry over high heat for 2 minutes, tossing and shaking the pan constantly.

7 Add the sweetbreads to the pan and toss to mix with the mushrooms. Pour in the reduced cooking liquid and bring to the boil, stirring. Lower the heat and slowly stir in the cream. Heat through gently, then stir in the basil, with salt and pepper to taste. Transfer to a warmed serving dish, garnish with basil sprigs and serve immediately.

Menu Suggestion
Sweetbreads prepared and cooked in this way are absolutely delicious. Even if your guests haven't tried them before, they are bound to like them cooked with such familiar—and good—ingredients as mushrooms and cream. The dish is quite rich, so serve in a ring of boiled rice, accompanied by a simple salad.

USEFUL INFORMATION AND BASIC RECIPES

Guide to Cuts, Cooking Methods and Techniques

In this chapter you will find information on all the different cuts of lamb and pork, with tips for buying and storage. The best methods of cooking are also explained, with a useful roasting chart giving cooking times and temperatures for the most common cuts. Plus techniques of meat preparation, such as boning, and information on the best equipment for the job.

LAMB

Leg An excellent roasting joint comprising lean meat with a thin covering of fat and skin. Can be cooked on the bone, or boned, rolled and stuffed. Often divided in half to form the fillet end and the knuckle half leg or shank end. Leg slices approximately 1 cm ($\frac{1}{2}$ inch) thick are also available; these can be used for grilling or braising or cubed for kebabs.

Shoulder A succulent, tender roasting joint containing a fair proportion of bone and fat. Sold whole or halved into blade and knuckle. Shoulder can be a difficult cut to carve, so for convenience it is often boned, stuffed and rolled. The meat can also be cubed for kebabs and casseroles. The blade half of the shoulder makes a good small roasting joint, while the knuckle half has more bone and is more useful for braising.

Loin A prime lean joint either for roasting in the piece, or for boning and stuffing. Loin is usually divided into loin end and chump end, and cut into chops for grilling and frying. Chump chops are recognisable by the small round bone in the centre. Loin chump ends are the end pieces of chump which tend to be bony but make an economical cut for braising with vegetables.

Best End of Neck Can be purchased as a roasting joint with a row of 6 or 8 rib bones. The butcher will chine or chop the back bone if requested, to make carving easier. Can be roasted on the bone or boned, stuffed and rolled. Two best end necks joined together and curved, bones outwards, make a Crown Roast. Facing each other, fat side outwards, they make a Guard of Honour. Both these special occasion dishes can be stuffed before roasting. Best end of neck chops are small chops cut between the rib bones.

Scrag and Middle Neck Usually sold as chops on the bone and used for stewing and braising. Traditional cuts for Lancashire Hot Pot and Irish Stew.

Neck Fillet Tender, boneless strip of meat taken from the neck of large lambs. Use for kebabs, curries, casseroles, grilling and frying.

Breast Long thin cut, streaked with fat and lean. When boned, rolled and stuffed, it makes an economical cut for roasting and braising. Cut into riblets, can be cooked in a barbecue sauce as for pork spareribs (page 132), after simmering in stock to tenderise.

Minced Lamb Lean minced lamb for use in moussaka, pies, burgers, patties, etc.

OFFAL

Lamb's Liver Has a good flavour, fine texture and is very tender. Can be grilled, fried or casseroled. Avoid overcooking, which toughens the meat.

Lamb's Kidneys Are small, about 50–75 g (2–3 oz) each, and are ideal for grills and quick frying. Need careful cooking as easily become tough when cooked for too long. Allow 2–3 kidneys per portion.

Lamb's Hearts Need to be cooked long and slow, and make flavoursome, economical meals. The meat is very lean and is best stewed or braised to prevent it becoming dry. Serve 1 lamb's heart per portion.

Lamb's Tongues A little fiddly to prepare, but very good hot or cold. Should be soaked in salted water for 2–3 hours before cooking, then simmered for $2\frac{1}{2}$–3 hours. The tongues should then be skinned before serving.

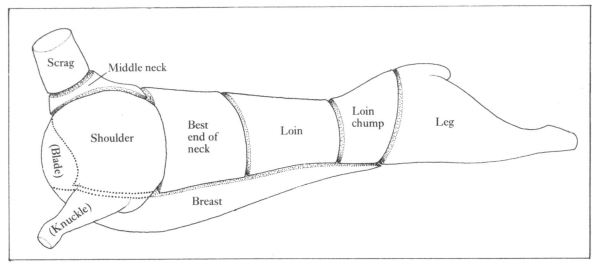

Major cuts of lamb to be found at your butcher

Lamb's Sweetbreads Have a delicate texture and flavour and must always be sold very fresh or frozen. After soaking for several hours, changing the salted water occasionally, they are simmered in flavoured milk or stock for 8–10 minutes. The cooking liquid can then be made into a sauce to accompany the sweetbreads. Alternatively, they can be braised or coated in egg and crumbs before frying.

CHOOSING AND BUYING LAMB

Look for fine-grained, lean meat with a bright red colour tinged with brown. The fat should be creamy white, and not brittle. The bones should be moist and white at the joints. Legs and shoulders should have a thin covering of fat. The fat of some cuts is covered with a thin papery skin. This should be pliable, not hard and wrinkled. Remove from chops before cooking, but leave on roasting joints as it helps the meat to retain moisture. English new season's lamb is available between March and November, although supplies are at their peak between August and November. All joints, except those from the neck, can be roasted, and the individual cuts from them grilled or fried.

STORING LAMB

Freshly cut meat should be stored in a cool place, preferably in the refrigerator. Minced lamb should be used within 24 hours. If no

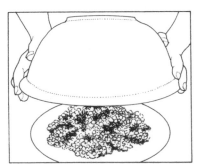

Cover mince with bowl to store

refrigerator is available, place the meat on a plate in a cool place and cover with an upturned large bowl. In a refrigerator, wrap the meat in foil or cling film. Never leave fresh meat in the sealed polythene bag in which it was bought. It should be placed on the shelf below the frozen food compartment. Lamb can be stored for up to 4 days in the refrigerator.

PORK

Neck End A large, economical roasting joint, particularly good when boned, stuffed and rolled. Often divided into blade and sparerib. These 2 smaller cuts can also be roasted, braised or stewed. Boned sparerib makes the best filling for pies. Sparerib chops are suitable for braising, and for slow grilling and frying.

Hand and Spring A large roasting joint, often divided into smaller cuts, hand and shank. As well as being suitable for roasting, hand and shank can be used for casseroles and stews.

Belly A long thin cut with streaks of fat and lean. Stuffed thick end of belly makes an economical roast. Belly is sometimes rather fat, and is better used sliced for grilling and frying rather than braising and stewing.

Leg Can be cut into 4 or more succulent roasting joints, often divided into fillet end and knuckle end. Fillet end is the prime roasting joint, which can be boned and stuffed. Sometimes sliced into steaks for grilling and frying.

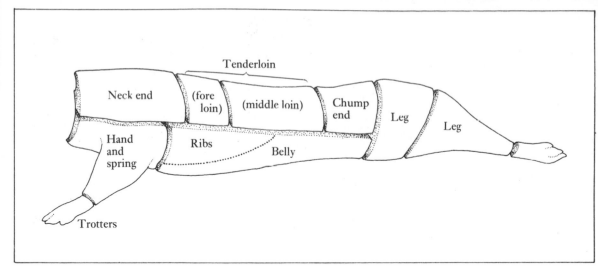

Major cuts of pork to be found at your butcher

Loin A popular roast on the bone, or boned and rolled. Often divided into loin chops, with or without kidney, and large chump chops. Both these chops are very good grilled, fried or baked. Loin of pork produces good crackling.

Tenderloin A tender, lean cut from underneath the back bone of the loin. Sometimes called pork fillet. Can be stuffed and rolled for roasting, cubed for kebabs or grilled. Can also be cut into slices or cubes for frying.

Trotters (feet) Usually salted and boiled and used to make brawn. They are also used to make a flavoursome gelatinous stock.

Ribs Rib bones with a thin covering of lean and fat. Use for barbecued spareribs. Sometimes also called Chinese spareribs.

Knuckle A large bone, covered with meat and rind. Used mainly for enriching slow-cooking casseroles, and as an addition to braised meats.

OFFAL

Pig's Liver Darker in colour and stronger in flavour than lamb's liver. Can be soaked for 1–2 hours in salted water or milk, to reduce the strong taste. Cook as for lamb's liver, or use in pâtés, terrines, faggots, etc.

Pig's Kidneys Similar to lamb's, but slightly larger and with a stronger flavour and firmer texture. Soak in salted water for several hours to reduce the strong taste. Grill, fry or slice and add to casseroles and hot pots. When grilling or frying, time the cooking carefully to avoid overcooking.

Pig's Hearts Larger than lamb's, weighing 8 oz–1 lb (225 g–450 g) each. Best stuffed and braised, or pot roasted, for 2–3 hours until tender. Serve ½–1 pig's heart per portion.

CHOOSING AND BUYING PORK

Good-quality pork is available all year round. Look for firm, dry lean meat with a good pinkish colour. The fat should be firm and creamy white. The rind should be smooth and supple. When deeply scored, the rind forms crackling on roast pork. Ask the butcher to score the meat if you want crackling.

STORING PORK

Pork is highly perishable, and should be eaten as soon after buying as possible. If no refrigerator is available, cook on the day of purchase. To store in a refrigerator, wrap in foil or cling film, to prevent the meat drying out. Never leave fresh meat in the sealed polythene bag in which it was bought. Cook within 2 days of purchase.

SALTING PORK

All cuts of pork, with the exception of loin, can be salted. If salt pork is not available from your butcher, it is very simple to prepare at home.

SALT PORK

1.8 kg (4 lb) piece pork
175 g (6 oz) coarse salt
30 ml (2 tbsp) brown sugar
15 ml (1 tbsp) juniper berries
4 cloves
3 bay leaves
1 blade mace
2 sprigs thyme

1 Wipe the meat with absorbent kitchen paper. Pour 1 litre (1¾ pints) water into a pan, add the salt and sugar and bring to the boil.

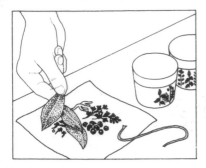

2 Wrap the spices and herbs in muslin and tie with string. Add to the liquid and boil for 2 minutes. Remove from heat and allow the brine to cool completely.

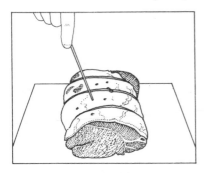

3 Remove the muslin bag. Prick the meat several times with a trussing needle. Place in a deep stoneware or earthenware crock. Pour the cold brine over the meat. Place a plate on top and weight down to keep the meat submerged. Cover the pot with a clean tea towel.

4 Stand the pot in a cool dark place, stirring every 2 days. Remove when sufficiently salted to your taste, from 3–7 days.

5 Before cooking, soak the meat in cold water for at least 3 hours, preferably overnight.

COOKING METHODS FOR LAMB AND PORK

There are no hard and fast rules for cooking meat, as each cut lends itself to a variety of treatments. However, the tender, leaner cuts are generally roasted or grilled, whereas the more economical, fattier cuts, which have more connective tissue, are usually more suitable for pot-roasting, braising or stewing. Before you start to cook, wipe the surface of the meat with damp absorbent kitchen paper. Trim off any excess fat, but do not remove it all as this helps with the flavour and moistness.

ROASTING

This is the most popular method of cooking large prime cuts of meat. It is only really suitable for cuts which have little connective tissue. Very lean meat will need added fat to prevent it from drying out. Lamb and pork are best roasted slowly to keep shrinkage to a minimum.

BASIC ROASTING METHOD

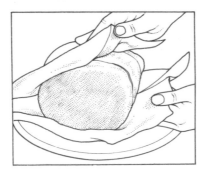

1 Wipe the meat with damp absorbent kitchen paper. Stand the meat on a rack if possible, in a roasting tin. Insert a meat thermometer, if available, into the centre of the thickest part of the joint, making sure the tip of the thermometer is clear of the bone.

2 Spread lamb joints that are particularly lean with a little lard, oil or butter. To make crackling, brush the scored rind of a joint of pork with oil, then rub in salt. Do not baste during cooking.

3 Cook in the oven at 180°C (350°F) mark 4 for the recommended time (see chart below). When ready, lift on to a warmed dish and leave to stand for 10–15 minutes. This makes carving easier and more economical. Meanwhile, make the gravy in the roasting tin (see page 145).

ROASTING CUTS, TEMPERATURES AND TIMES

PORK

Suitable cuts: loin; leg; shoulder; fore-end of hand; stuffed tenderloin; belly
Cooking temperature
180°C (350°F) mark 4. For crackling, increase temperature to 200°C (400°F) mark 6 for the last 20 minutes.
Cooking time
30 minutes per 450 g (1 lb) plus 30 minutes
Meat thermometer reading
80°C (180°F)
Classic Accompaniments
Sage and Onion Stuffing (page 148); Apple Sauce (page 148); gravy

LAMB

Suitable cuts: leg; shoulder; best end neck; loin; boned and rolled breast
Cooking temperature
180°C (350°F) mark 4
Cooking time
Medium: 25 minutes per 450 g (1 lb) plus 25 minutes
Well done: 30 minutes per 450 g (1 lb) plus 30 minutes
Meat thermometer reading
Medium: 70°C (160°F)
Well done: 80°C (180°F)
Classic Accompaniments
Mint Sauce (page 147); Mint Jelly (page 148); redcurrant jelly; Onion Sauce (page 148); gravy

SPIT ROASTING

The meat is placed on a revolving spit or skewers and cooked under a direct heat source, either in the oven or as a grill attachment. This method is suitable for any roasting joint, providing it is a uniform shape, well trussed and securely fastened to the spit. Normally, spit-roasted meats need no extra fat as they are self basting. Check your cooker instructions for cooking times.

BRAISING

Braising can be on top of the cooker, or in the oven. After browning in hot fat to seal the meat, it is placed on a bed of aromatic vegetables such as onion, carrot and celery, with just enough liquid to cover them. The pot is tightly covered and the meat cooks in the steam created by the liquid. After cooking, the meat is removed and the liquid boiled until reduced, then used to glaze the meat. The vegetables can be puréed to thicken the sauce.
Cooking temperature: 180°C (350°F) mark 4
Cooking time: 45 minutes per 450 g (1 lb)
    The following cuts are suitable for braising:
Pork: neck end; sparerib chops; liver; heart; kidney.
Lamb: middle neck; breast; shoulder; scrag; sweetbreads; heart; liver; kidney.

CASSEROLING AND STEWING

Less tender cuts of meat which are not suitable for grilling or roasting are best cooked slowly in liquid which can be water, stock, wine, cider or beer. Flavourings such as vegetables, herbs and spices, are added to give character to the dish. The meat should be cooked in no more than 300 ml ($\frac{1}{2}$ pint) liquid for each 450 g (1 lb) of meat and the liquid should be kept at a gentle simmer, never boiled. The casserole can be prepared either by the fry start method, where the meat and then the vegetables are browned in fat before adding the liquid, or by the cold start method in which the frying process is omitted and all the ingredients are brought slowly the boil.
Cooking temperature: 170°C (325°F) mark 3.
    The following cuts are suitable for stewing and casseroling:
Pork: hand and spring; shoulder; kidney.
Lamb: scrag; shoulder; middle neck; neck fillet; heart; liver; kidney; tongue.

FRYING

Only small pieces of tender, quick-cooking meats should be fried. It is therefore a good cooking method for chops, steaks, sausages and bacon, offal such as liver and kidney. Ideally, the meat to be fried should be no more than 2.5 cm (1 inch) thick. Use a large, heavy-based frying pan to ensure the meat cooks evenly. Have the fat preheated before adding the meat to seal in the juices quickly, then reduce the temperature to cook the meat through.
    Meat can be coated before frying to give a crisp surface and to protect the meat from drying in the hot fat. The cooking time varies according to the thickness of the meat, so the following is simply a rough guide:
2.5 cm (1 inch) thickness: 7–10 minutes
1 cm ($\frac{1}{2}$ inch) thickness: 4–5 minutes.
    The following cuts are suitable for frying:
Pork: loin chops; chump chops; sparerib chops; sliced belly; leg steaks; kidney; liver; tenderloin.
Lamb: best end neck cutlets; loin chops; chump chops; neck fillet; kidney; liver.

GRILLING

A quick-cooking method for tender cuts such as steaks, chops, sausages and bacon. As the heat is fierce, the meat often needs to be moistened with melted butter or oil before cooking. Grilling times vary according to the thickness of the meat and the preferred degree of cooking. Pork should always be thoroughly cooked through. Grilling always begins under high heat to help seal in the meat juices. The heat is then lowered to cook the meat further if necessary. Prepare the meat by wiping with

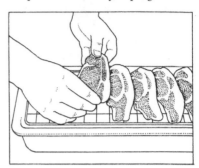

Grilling rashers of bacon

damp absorbent kitchen paper. Trim off any excess fat, or cut through the fat at regular intervals to prevent the meat from curling up during cooking. Brush with oil or melted butter and sprinkle with pepper. It is best to salt the meat when cooking is under way as salt draws out the natural meat juices.
    The following cuts are suitable for grilling:
Pork: loin chops; chump chops; sparerib chops; sliced belly; leg steaks; tenderloin; kidney; liver.
Lamb: best end neck cutlets; loin chops; chump chops; neck fillet; kidney; liver.

BOILING

This is a useful method of cooking less tender cuts, salted and cured meats and tongues. The meat is not really boiled, but gently simmered in water with root vegetables and sometimes herbs. The stock left over from cooking the meat makes an excellent base for soups and sauces. Salted meat for boiling should be soaked overnight or for at least 3 hours. If there is no time, place the meat in the pan with cold water to cover, bring slowly to the boil, skimming if necessary. Drain the meat and return it to a clean pan with water and root vegetables and proceed as usual.

Cooking times: Large salted joints should be cooked for 30 minutes per 450 g (1 lb) plus an extra 30 minutes. Small joints should be given a minimum of 1½ hours. Calculate the cooking time from the moment when the water reaches a simmer.

The following cuts of meat are suitable for boiling:
Pork: belly; hand and spring; tongue; head; cheek; trotters.
Lamb: tongue.

TECHNIQUES WITH LAMB AND PORK

Boning a piece of meat makes it easier to carve, and creates a useful cavity for the stuffing. Once you know how, it is not as complicated as you may think, and this section takes you through all the stages to ensure success. Other techniques of meat preparation are also covered.

EQUIPMENT

Choppers have heavy rectangular blades with strong edges. A heavy meat chopper will go through most bones and joints, but you may need a little practice to ensure you hit the right spot each time.

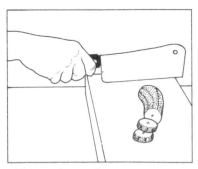

A heavy chopper has many uses

The technique is to use your fore arm and not your wrist and to look at the target, not the chopper. A chopper is also useful for flattening steaks and escalopes.

Butcher's knives are usually fairly heavy, with long, firm

blades. They are useful for slicing raw meat and for trimming and finishing joints before cooking.

Saws are used for cutting a carcass and are the only tool which will cut through any bone. A hacksaw will cut through most smaller bones, but with a butcher's bow saw you would be able to cut up a carcass yourself, although this is rarely necessary. When sawing through bone, remove any dust from the meat immediately.

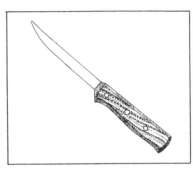

A knife for removing bones

Boning knives are used for removing bones from raw meat and poultry. They are smallish knives, with small sharp pointed blades. The knife should be kept very sharp for maximum efficiency.

Skewers hold meat firmly in shape during cooking. Both wooden and metal skewers are available in various sizes. Kebab

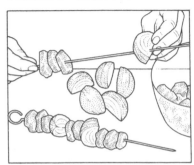

Steel skewers are used for kebabs

skewers are made of flat strips of steel to prevent the food from swinging round while being barbecued or grilled.

Larding needles have sharp points and long hollow bodies for threading small strips of fat through very lean meat. These are rarely used these days as modern cooking techniques prevent meat from drying out during cooking.

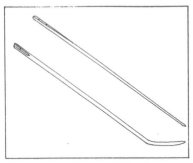

Trussing needles should be sharp

Trussing needles are like very large darning needles. The eye must be large enough to take fine string and the point should be very sharp. They are useful for tying up meat and sewing up stuffed joints. Check you thread enough string on to the needle to complete the job.

HOW TO TIE UP A JOINT

1 Gather or roll the meat to a neat shape. Cut a piece of fine string to a suitable length.

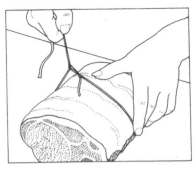

2 Slide the string under the joint and make a loop in one end. Thread other end through the loop and pull ends to tighten.

3 Tie a knot and cut off the ends of the string. Repeat at 2.5–5 cm (1–2 inch) intervals.

HOW TO BONE A LEG OF LAMB OR PORK

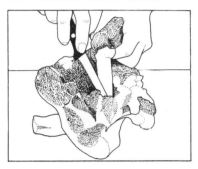

1 Starting from the fillet end, cut around the bone. Scrape the meat from the bone, rolling back the flesh as you go. Continue until the joint is reached.

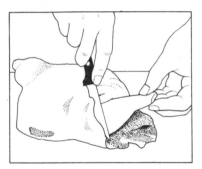

2 Turn the meat round and cut around the shank end to release the meat from the bone. Continue working down the meat, rolling back the flesh from the joint, then pull out the bone.

3 Fill the cavity with chosen stuffing, if used. Skewer the joint or tie into a neat shape with string or trussing thread.

HOW TO BONE A SHOULDER OF LAMB

1 Follow the same method as for boning a leg of lamb, starting by freeing the meat from the flat blade bone. Scrape the meat away from the bone, rolling it back until you reach the joint.

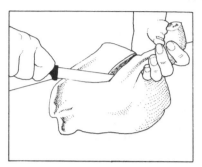

2 Turn the joint around and free the meat from around the shank bone. If necessary, split the flesh up to the bone a little to make it easier. Scrape the flesh away from the shank end until the joint is reached.

3 Pull the bone out from the cavity and add the stuffing. Tie or skewer into a neat shape.

HOW TO BONE A BREAST OF LAMB

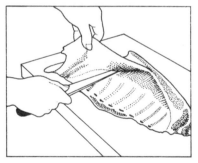

1 Place the breast skin side down on a board. Cut along the flap of meat over the bones and pull back to reveal the bones. Carefully cut around each bone using a small sharp pointed knife.

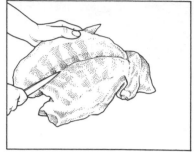

2 Working from one end, scrape away the meat from each bone. Lift the bones from the meat. Trim off excess fat and skin.

3 Turn the meat over and remove the skin by cutting between the skin and fat, pulling the skin away with the other hand.

4 Turn the meat over again and spread evenly with stuffing. Roll up from one long edge. Tie neatly at intervals with trussing string into an even shape.

HOW TO BONE A LOIN OF PORK

1 Remove the kidney if necessary. Place the loin on a board with the skin side down. Trim away any loose fat.

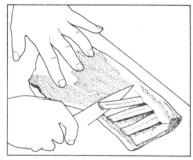

2 Cut along both sides of one rib at a time. Gently pull the rib upwards away from the meat and insert the knife under the bone. Work down the bone to free it from the meat.

3 Twist the bone sharply to break it away from the spine. Repeat with each rib.

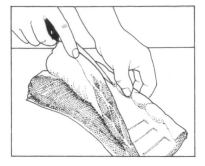

4 Remove the fillet from the spine through the strip of connective tissue. Keep the knife close to the spine as you go.

5 Work down the spine with the point of the knife to free it from the meat. Stuff thc joint, roll it up firmly and tie into a neat shape with trussing string.

HOW TO MAKE A GUARD OF HONOUR

1 You will need 2 best end necks of lamb (sometimes called racks of lamb). Place them skin side up on a board. With the point of a sharp knife, remove the thin piece of bone from one end of each rack of lamb.

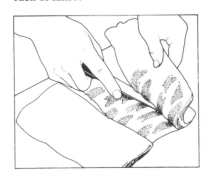

2 Score a straight line across each rack, about 7.5 cm (3 inches) from the tips of the bones. Remove the layer of fat and meat between the scored line and the bone tips. Cut out the meat from between each bone. Scrape the bones clean of meat and fat.

3 Place the bones flat on the board. Using a heavy knife, cut each tip diagonally.

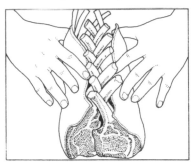

4 Place the 2 racks up, concave sides facing each other. Press them together, interlacing the bone ends. Tie in 3 places.

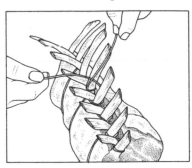

5 With a long piece of string, interlace the bone ends, tying them firmly at the end. The cavity may be filled with stuffing.

HOW TO PREPARE NOISETTES OF LAMB

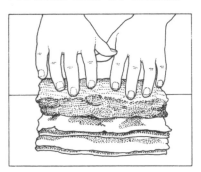

1 Bone out a best end of neck, following the instructions given for boning a loin of pork. Roll the meat up tightly, starting from the eye of meat.

2 Tie the lamb roll neatly at 2.5 cm (1 inch) intervals, using fine string. Cut between each piece of string to make noisettes.

HOW TP PREPARE KIDNEYS

1 Remove fat (suet) if still attached. Remove fine membrane around the kidney.

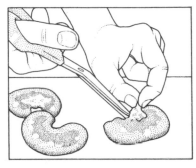

2 Cut each kidney almost in half from rounded side to core. Snip out white core with scissors.

3 Wash the kidneys well. Soak in salted water for 15 minutes, then drain and pat dry.

HOW TO PREPARE A HEART

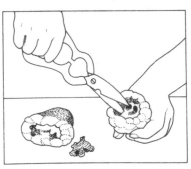

1 Wash heart in water to remove any blood. Snip out the arteries and tendons. Soak in salted water for 15 minutes, then drain and pat dry. Stuff heart if liked, then sew up.

Carving

For many of us, carving meat on the bone is a daunting prospect. Knowing where to locate the bones and using the right equipment will give you confidence and, as always, practice makes perfect. Traditionally, lamb and pork are carved into fairly thick slices, and the meat is carved across the grain for maximum tenderness.

THE RIGHT TOOLS

The essential tools for correct carving are a two-pronged carving fork with a finger guard, a large sharp carving knife and an efficient knife sharpener.

SHARPENING A KNIFE USING A STEEL

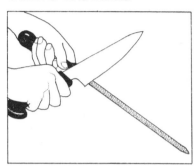

1 Keep the blade of the knife at a 30° angle to the steel and bring the whole length of the edge in contact with it. Use your wrist and forearm, keeping your elbow still. Start with the heel of the knife by the guard, and end with the point at the tip of the steel.

2 Sharpen the other side of the blade under the steel. About 10–12 strokes should be sufficient to sharpen the knife.

HOW TO CARVE A LEG OF LAMB

1 Use a cloth or absorbent kitchen paper to hold the shank end of the joint and place the meatiest side uppermost.

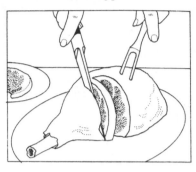

2 Take out 2 slices from the centre of the leg down to the bone. Continue slicing from either side of the first cut, gradually angling the knife to obtain larger slices.

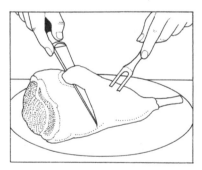

3 Turn the joint over and trim off excess fat. Carve horizontal slices along the leg.

TIPS FOR EASY CARVING
- Boned and rolled joints are simply sliced through. Small flat joints are easier to carve horizontally.
- Ask the butcher to chine a loin of lamb or pork. The bone can then be easily removed before carving, making the meat easier to slice.
- Leave the joint to rest for 10–15 minutes before carving. This firms up the meat and makes it easier to carve neatly.
- Always carve on a non-slip surface. A damp cloth placed under the board helps to keep it steady.
- As far as possible, loosen the cooked meat from exposed bones, such as rib bones, before starting to carve. Remove some or all the crackling from pork and cut it up separately.
- Aim to cut across the grain of the meat. This usually means at right angles to the bone.

HOW TO CARVE A SHOULDER OF LAMB

1 Use a cloth or absorbent kitchen paper to hold the shank end of the joint and place the meatiest side uppermost.

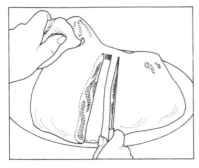

2 Cut a long slice from the centre of the joint down to the bone. Carve thick slices from either side of the initial cut.

3 Carve horizontal slices from the shank bone. Turn the joint over and trim off any excess fat. Carve thin horizontal slices from the remaining meat.

HOW TO CARVE A LOIN OF PORK

1 Remove the crackling from the loin of pork in sections, using a sharp knife.

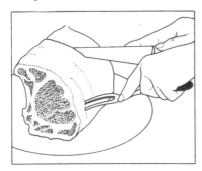

2 Slice the loin, working at a slight angle, cutting down to the bone.

HOW TO CARVE A HAND OF PORK

1 Remove the crackling and detach the rib bones.

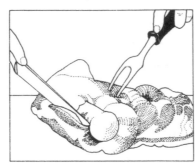

2 Carve downward slices, working from either side of the bone.

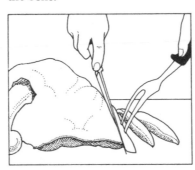

3 Turn the joint over and trim off excess fat. Carve the remaining meat across the grain.

HOW TO CARVE A LEG OF PORK (KNUCKLE END)

1 First, remove the crackling from the knuckle end of pork in sections.

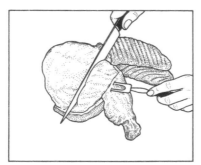

2 Start carving on the thick side at the knuckle end, slice at a slight angle down the bone.

HOW TO CARVE A LEG OF PORK (FILLET END)

1 First, remove the crackling from the fillet end of pork in pieces.

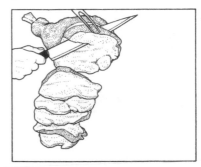

2 Place the joint flat, with the thick side on the right. Carve a few slices from the thick edge towards the centre bone, then turn the joint so that the thin side is on the right and carve in towards the bone until the surface is level.

3 Continue carving the meat, keeping the surfaces as level as possible.

HOW TO CARVE BELLY OF PORK

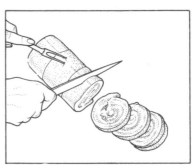

1 Place flat, fat side uppermost and carve downwards in fairly thick slices across the grain of the meat. If boned, rolled and stuffed, carve in the same way.

Guide to Bacon, Gammon and Ham

Meat was originally cured to provide food during the long winters when little fresh meat was available. It was discovered that pork was easier to salt than beef, as the flesh of the smaller animal was penetrated more easily by the curing salts. Nowadays we eat bacon, gammon and ham purely for the good flavour and to give variety.

BACON

Bacon is cured from the sides and back of a pig, bred specially for its lean meat. All bacon is preserved in salt and it can then be smoked, or left unsmoked. Unsmoked, or green, bacon has a pale rind and pink flesh. Smoked bacon has a golden-brown rind and a darker pink flesh than unsmoked.

GAMMON AND HAM

Gammon is the name given to the entire hind leg of a bacon pig after curing. When cooked and served cold, it is usually called ham. Speciality hams, such as York Ham, are produced from whole legs separated from the carcass before being cured and cooked by traditional methods. Cooked ham is sold freshly sliced or as vacuum-packed slices. Uncooked gammon is usually sold as joints or steaks.

CUTS OF BACON

Back Prime back is sliced into rashers or thicker chops. It can be grilled, fried or baked. It can also be bought as one piece for boiling or braising. Long back is usually sliced into rashers and can be used for grilling and frying.

Collar A more economical joint which is best boiled or braised. It is also sliced into rashers.

Forehock A good joint for casseroling, or the meat can be removed from the bone and used in stews and casseroles.

Middle or Through Cut Back and streaky together, giving a double piece with a good proportion of fat and lean. Cut into rashers, it is grilled and fried. As a joint, it is good stuffed and rolled for baking.

Streaky A good mixture of lean and fat. It can be bought in the piece for boiling and is delicious cold. Thinly sliced streaky rashers can be grilled or fried.

Gammon Is the prime cut of bacon. As it is a large piece it is generally cut into 3 joints. The middle gammon is lean and meaty; gammon rashers and steaks are cut from this piece. It can be boiled, braised or roasted. Corner gammon is a small, triangular-shaped piece. It is best boiled for serving hot or cold. Gammon hock is a large piece with a large bone, but also plenty of lean meat. It can be boiled, baked or braised.

BUYING BACON

Bacon should have a pleasant smell, with no stickiness. The rind should be thin and smooth, and the fat smooth and white. Bacon can be bought ready boned and rolled into convenient-sized joints, or it can be cling film wrapped or vacuum packed. Some joints are also sold in convenient boilable bags.

STORING BACON

Wrap bacon joints in foil and store in the refrigerator for up to 3 days. Green, or unsmoked, bacon rashers can be stored for up to 7 days, smoked for up to 10 days. Wrap in foil or place in a covered plastic food container. Cooked bacon joints can be stored in the refrigerator for up to 4 days.

PREPARING BACON FOR COOKING

Mild-cured bacon needs little preparation. It is not over salty and it is usually not necessary to soak it. Other joints should be soaked for 3 hours for unsmoked, and 6 hours or overnight for smoked. To soak: place the joint in a large bowl or saucepan and cover it with cold water. After soaking for the correct time, drain off and discard the water. Use fresh water for boiling the joint.

To prepare rashers, steaks and

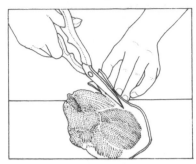

Remove bacon rind with scissors

chops: remove the rind with scissors, or snip through the rind and fat around thick rashers, steaks and bacon chops to prevent curling. Remove any small bones.

COOKING METHODS FOR BACON

Joints of bacon can be boiled, baked or braised. Rashers, chops and steaks are grilled or fried.

BOILING

1 Soak the joint if necessary for the correct time. Discard the soaking liquid.

2 Weigh the joint and calculate the cooking time. Allow 30 minutes per 450 g (1 lb) for joints up to 4.5 kg (10 lb) and 25 minutes per 450 g (1 lb) if larger.

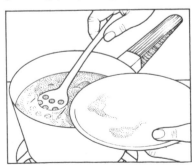

3 Place in a saucepan and add water to cover. Bring slowly to the boil. Remove any scum with a slotted spoon.

4 Time the cooking from the moment when the water reaches boiling point. Cover and simmer for the calculated time.

5 Remove the bacon from the pan and rest for 10 minutes before slicing.

BAKING

1 Prepare the joint as above and calculate the cooking time as for boiling. Put in a pan, cover with water and simmer for half the calculated cooking time. Drain.

2 Wrap the drained joint in foil and place in a roasting tin. Bake in the oven at 180°C (350°F) mark 4 for the remainder of the calculated cooking time.

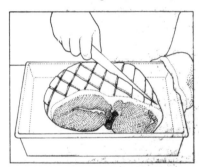

3 If you wish to glaze the joint, remove the foil 30 minutes before the end of the cooking time. Strip off the rind and score the fat into diamonds with a sharp knife.

4 Glaze with any of the following and return to the oven for the remaining cooking time: 30 ml (2 tbsp) brown sugar and 10 ml (2 tsp) mustard powder mixed together; honey; marmalade (orange, lemon, lemon and lime, ginger); pieces of canned apricots or pineapple, basting with the juices from the can.

BRAISING

1 Melt a little fat in a flameproof casserole large enough to take the joint comfortably. Lightly fry a selection of root vegetables.

2 Cover the vegetables with stock or cider and bring to the boil. Place the bacon joint on top and cover the pan tightly. Braise in the oven at 180°C (350°F) mark 4 for 30 minutes per 450 g (1 lb) for joints up to 4.5 kg (10 lb), and 25 minutes per 450 g (1 lb) if the joint is larger.

3 Thirty minutes before the end of the calculated cooking time, remove the rind from the joint and return the casserole to the oven, uncovered.

4 Thicken the cooking liquid with a little blended cornflour before serving with the bacon.

GRILLING RASHERS

1 Preheat the grill to hot. Arrange the rashers on the grill rack, with the fat over the lean.

2 Put under the preheated hot grill for 3–5 minutes, depending on the thickness of the rashers and crispness required. Turn halfway through the cooking time. Drain on absorbent kitchen paper before serving.

GRILLING STEAKS AND CHOPS

1 Preheat the grill to hot. Place the steaks or chops on the grill pan rack.

2 Brush the lean with melted fat or oil. Put under the preheated hot grill and cook for 12–15 minutes for chops; 10–12 minutes for steaks. Reduce the heat and turn the bacon over halfway through the cooking time.

FRYING RASHERS

1 Place the rashers in a cold frying pan. Overlap back rashers with the fat under the lean.

2 Heat the pan gently. To crisp the rashers, increase the heat. Cook for 3–5 minutes, turning the rashers over halfway.

Freezing

A supply of meat in the freezer is convenient for a family, cuts down on shopping trips, and can save money if you bulk buy a whole or half carcass. This chapter tells you all about buying, freezing and storing pork and lamb to suit your needs and space available.

HOW TO BUY LAMB AND PORK FOR THE FREEZER

Meat on the bone takes up roughly twice as much freezer space as boneless meat. So if space is limited, you may find it worthwhile to pay more for prepared joints. As a general guide, the chart below gives the amount of freezer space required.

It makes sense only to buy as much meat as can reasonably be used during the recommended storage time. However, meat kept after this time need not be destroyed. It is perfectly safe to eat, but its flavour and texture will deteriorate progressively the longer it is kept.

THE BEST TIME TO BUY

As meat is a natural product, there are seasonal fluctuations in the quality available. The best time to buy meat for the freezer is when there is peak supply but low demand, causing the price to be low. Pork is less seasonal than lamb or beef, although supplies tend to fall off due to a drop in demand during hot weather, which can be a good time to bulk buy. In the UK prices tend to go up from September to Christmas as demand increases, but supplies remain fairly constant. Home-produced lambs mature from March onwards. Early in the season, lamb is expensive as supplies are low. Prices tend to fall in the late summer or autumn when production is at its peak.

WHERE TO BUY MEAT FOR THE FREEZER

Butchers specialising in meat for the freezer will cut and pack the meat to your exact requirements, then supply it fresh, or freeze it for you, whichever you prefer. It is also worthwhile checking if there is a delivery service. Carcasses, part carcasses, selected cuts and mixed meats are often available at considerable discounts. Ready frozen meat is available from freezer food centres, specialist frozen meat suppliers and most large supermarkets. They usually offer carcasses, side or quarters, cut to their own specifications. Also single cut packs of joints, steaks or chops as well as mince and offal. A side of lamb or pork will provide varying amounts of roasting, stewing and braising meat, as well as mince, chops and steaks. Cuts from larger animals of 16–18 kg (36–40 lb) total weight will usually be too large for the average small family; it is better to choose a 11–12 kg (26–28 lb) carcass weight if small joints are preferred.

FREEZING BACON AND HAM

Pork fat turns rancid more quickly than beef or lamb. The presence of salt in bacon and ham accelerates the development of rancidity, thus shortening the storage life of bacon and ham compared with uncured pork. It is not advisable to freeze uncooked salt pork because storage life is unpredictable and generally short.

Vacuum packing considerably

	Average gross weight	Prepared weight	Freezer space required
Lamb–whole carcass	16 kg (35 lb)	13.5 kg (30 lb)	42.5 cubic mm (1½ cubic feet)
Pork–half carcass	22.5 kg (50 lb)	20.5 kg (45 lb)	56.5 cubic mm (2 cubic feet)

increases the freezer life of bacon. Prepacked bacon or joints are vacuum sealed and can simply be overwrapped with polythene before freezing.

PACKING FRESH MEAT FOR THE FREEZER

Unless meat is well protected from the extreme cold of the freezer, it will dehydrate and deteriorate quickly. It must be protected by wrapping closely in tough, moisture- and vapour-proof material.

The effect of dehydration on badly wrapped food is freezer burn, which changes the colour, texture and flavour of the food. It shows as greyish white marks on the surface of poultry, meat and fish. It can also occur when food is stored for too long. Although safe to eat, the food will not be such a good flavour as well stored food, and it may also be rather dry.

SUITABLE FREEZER WRAPPINGS

Double aluminium foil or **heavy duty foil** can be moulded closely around meat and needs no special sealing.

Extra thick polythene bags or **freezer bags**. As much air as possible should be excluded from bags, which should then be securely tied.

Boil-in-bags are useful for small quantities of items such as cooked meat sauce or stews. These are special high density polythene bags in which food may be frozen and cooked.

Cling film is useful for interleaving chops, sausages and steaks, to enable them to be easily separated. They should then be overwrapped with polythene or freezer film.

All food must be clearly labelled with the type, quantity and date of freezing.

MAXIMUM FREEZER STORAGE TIMES FOR LAMB AND PORK

Uncooked lamb	9 months
Uncooked pork	6 months
Sausages	3 months
Casseroles	6 months
Curries	4 months
Pies	3 months
Stock	6 months

MAXIMUM FREEZER STORAGE TIMES FOR BACON AND HAM

Bacon joints (smoked and unsmoked)	1 month
Vacuum-packed bacon joints	3 months
Bacon rashers, steaks and chops (smoked and unsmoked)	1 month
Vacuum-packed bacon rashers, steaks and chops	6 months
Cooked ham, loose	1 month
Cooked ham, vacuum packed	6 months
Casseroles containing bacon	1 month
Pâté containing bacon	1 month

THAWING TIMES

	In refrigerator
Joints 1.5 kg (3 lb) plus	6–7 hours per 450 g (1 lb)
Joints under 1.5 kg (3 lb)	3–4 hours per 450 g (1 lb)
Steaks, chops, etc.	5–6 hours

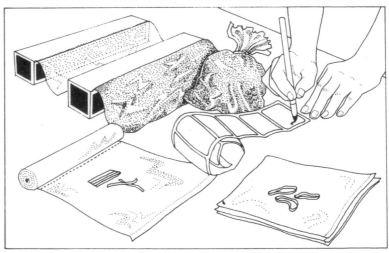

It is important to pack and label meat carefully before freezing

Sauces and Flavourings

There are many ways to flavour and enhance lamb and pork dishes. Home-made stocks, glazes — especially for ham and bacon joints — and marinades add flavour to meat: marinades also tenderise. A variety of mouthwatering stuffing recipes are included — stuffings not only flavour meat but extend it, too, making many meals more economical.

Accompanying traditional sauces can be found in this chapter, together with instructions for making perfect gravy.

LAMB STOCK

Makes about 1.4 litres (2½ pints)

900 g (2 lb) lamb scraps (eg shank, middle neck or scrag), cut into pieces
450 g (1 lb) lamb bones, chopped
1 onion, skinned and sliced
1 carrot, peeled and sliced
1 celery stick, trimmed and sliced
15 ml (1 tbsp) tomato purée (optional)
1 bouquet garni
6 black peppercorns

1 Put the meat, bones and vegetables in a roasting tin. Brown in the oven at 200°C (400°F) mark 6 for 30–40 minutes, stirring frequently.

2 With a slotted spoon, transfer to a large saucepan. Cover with 1.7 litres (3 pints) cold water, add the tomato purée, if liked, the bouquet garni and peppercorns. Bring to the boil.

3 Skim off any scum that forms with a slotted spoon. Half cover the pan and simmer very gently for 5–6 hours.

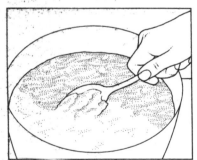

4 Strain the stock into a bowl. Leave until cold, then lift off any fat that has risen and set on the surface.

5 Cover and chill until required. Store for up to 4 days. It can be kept for longer but should then be boiled for at least 10 minutes, every day.

CHICKEN STOCK

Use in lamb or pork dishes

Makes 1.1–1.4 litres (2–2½ pints)

carcass and bones of a cooked or raw chicken, and any chicken scraps
1 onion, skinned and sliced
1 carrot, peeled and sliced
1 celery stick, trimmed and sliced
6 black peppercorns
1 bouquet garni

1 Break down the carcass and bones of the chicken, and make sure to include any skin and chicken scraps.

2 Put in a large saucepan with 1.4–1.7 litres (2½–3 pints) cold water, the onion, carrot, celery, peppercorns and bouquet garni. Bring to the boil.

3 Skim off any scum that forms with a slotted spoon. Half cover the pan and simmer very gently for about 3 hours.

4 Strain the stock into a bowl. Leave until cold, then lift off any fat that has risen to the surface.

5 Cover and chill until required. Store for up to 4 days. It can be kept for longer but should then be boiled for at least 10 minutes, every day.

WHITE STOCK
Use in pork dishes

Makes about 1.7 litres (3 pints)

900 g (2 lb) knuckle of veal, chopped

juice of ½ lemon

2 carrots, peeled and sliced

1 onion, skinned and sliced

1 bouquet garni

6 black peppercorns

1 Put the bones in a large saucepan with 2.3 litres (4 pints) cold water. Add the lemon juice and bring to the boil.

2 Skim off any scum that forms with a slotted spoon. Add the vegetables, bouquet garni and peppercorns and bring back to the boil. Half cover the pan and simmer for 5–6 hours.

3 Strain the stock into a bowl. Leave until cold, then lift off any fat that has risen to the surface.

4 Cover and chill until required. Store for up to 4 days. It can be kept for longer but should then be boiled for at least 10 minutes, every day.

MEAT GLAZE
Makes about 150 ml (¼ pint) glaze

4.5 litres (1 gallon) good stock

1 Skim the stock and pour into a strong saucepan. Bring to the boil and continue boiling for several hours, until reduced to the consistency of a glaze.

2 Leave to cool, then pour into a bowl, cover and store in the refrigerator. It will keep for several months.

3 For enriching gravies and sauces, reconstitute by adding up to 5 ml (1 tsp) glaze per 600 ml (1 pint) liquid.

GRAVY

A rich brown gravy is served with all roast joints. If the gravy is properly made in the roasting tin, there should be no need to use gravy powders or mixes, or extra colouring.

Remove the joint from the tin and allow it to stand while making the gravy.

THIN GRAVY

1 Pour the fat very slowly from the roasting tin, draining it off carefully from one corner and leaving the sediment behind.

2 Add plenty of salt and pepper to the sediment in the tin. Pour in 300 ml (½ pint) hot vegetable water or stock (which can be made from a stock cube). Stir thoroughly with a wooden spoon until all the sediment is scraped from the tin and the gravy is a rich brown.

3 Place the tin on top of the cooker, bring to the boil, stirring, then simmer for 2–3 minutes. Serve very hot.

This is the 'correct' way of making thin gravy, but some people prefer to make a version of the thick gravy given above right, using half the amount of flour.

THICK GRAVY

1 Pour the fat very slowly from the roasting tin as for thin gravy (left), but leaving behind 30 ml (2 tbsp) of the fat.

2 Using a flour dredger to give a smooth result, shake in about 15 ml (1 tbsp) plain flour for pork gravy, about 7.5 ml (½ tbsp) for lamb gravy.

3 Blend well with a wooden spoon and cook over the heat until brown, stirring constantly. Slowly stir in 300 ml (½ pint) hot vegetable water or stock, bring to the boil, then simmer for 2–3 minutes. Add plenty of salt and pepper to taste, strain and serve very hot.

NOTES

1 If the gravy is greasy (due to not draining off enough fat) or thin (due to adding too much liquid), it can be corrected by adding more flour, although this weakens the flavour.

2 When gravy is very pale, a little gravy browning may be added for colour.

3 For extra flavour, meat extracts are sometimes added to gravy, but they do tend to overpower the characteristic meat flavour. A sliced carrot and onion cooked with meat in the gravy will give extra 'body' to the taste without impairing it, and 15 ml (1 tbsp) cider or wine added at the last moment is excellent.

GLAZES FOR BAKED HAM OR BACON

SPICED MARMALADE AND HONEY GLAZE

Makes enough to glaze a 2 kg (4½ lb) joint

60 ml (4 tbsp) fine shred marmalade
75 ml (5 tbsp) clear honey
4–5 drops Tabasco sauce

1 Blend the marmalade, honey and Tabasco sauce together in a bowl.

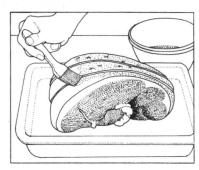

2 Brush about one-third of the glaze over the joint 30 minutes before the end of the cooking time.

3 Bake for 10 minutes, then brush with another third of the glaze; bake for a further 10 minutes, then repeat with the last of the glaze. Do not use the glaze that has run into the tin as this will dull the shine.

SHARP HONEY GLAZE

Makes enough to glaze a 2 kg (4½ lb) joint

15 ml (1 tbsp) clear honey
30 ml (2 tbsp) vinegar
50 g (2 oz) brown sugar
50 g (2 oz) fresh white breadcrumbs

1 Warm the honey and vinegar together in a small saucepan until the honey has melted.

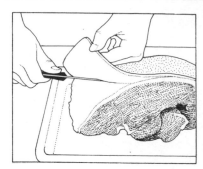

2 Strip the rind off the bacon and pour the sharp honey glaze over the fat (as in recipe above).

3 Mix the sugar and breadcrumbs together and sprinkle over the joint. Return to the oven and baste frequently until cooked.

SAVOURY BUTTERS

PARSLEY BUTTER (MAÎTRE D'HÔTEL)

Serve with grilled lamb and pork

125 g (4 oz) butter
30 ml (2 tbsp) finely chopped fresh parsley
good squeeze of lemon juice
salt
cayenne pepper

1 Put the butter in a bowl and beat until soft and creamy. Add the remaining ingredients and beat again until combined.

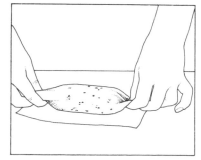

2 Shape the butter into a roll and wrap in greaseproof paper or foil. Chill for 2–3 hours until firm. Use within 2–3 weeks.

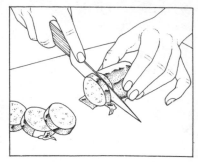

3 To serve, cut into pats about 0.5 cm (¼ inch) thick. Use well chilled or the butter will melt too quickly on the hot meat.

───── VARIATIONS ─────

GARLIC BUTTER

125 g (4 oz) butter
2 garlic cloves, skinned and crushed
salt and freshly ground pepper

FRESH HERB BUTTER

125 g (4 oz) butter
5 ml (1 tsp) chopped fresh tarragon
5 ml (1 tsp) chopped fresh parsley
5 ml (1 tsp) finely grated onion
salt and freshly ground pepper

Note These herbs may be varied according to season.

ORANGE AND PARSLEY BUTTER

125 g (4 oz) butter
finely grated rind of ½ orange
10 ml (2 tsp) orange juice
10 ml (2 tsp) chopped fresh parsley
salt and freshly ground pepper

GREEN BUTTER

125 g (4 oz) butter
50 g (2 oz) watercress, trimmed and finely chopped
salt and freshly ground pepper

ONION BUTTER

125 g (4 oz) butter
30 ml (2 tbsp) very finely chopped or grated onion
salt and freshly ground pepper

SAUCES TO SERVE WITH LAMB AND PORK

CUMBERLAND SAUCE

The classic accompaniment to lamb and ham

Serves 4

| 1 orange |
| 1 lemon |
| 60 ml (4 tbsp) redcurrant jelly |
| 60 ml (4 tbsp) port |
| 10 ml (2 tsp) arrowroot |

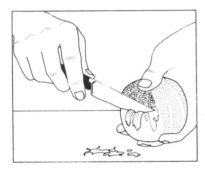

1 Pare the rind thinly from the orange and lemon, free of all the white pith.

2 Cut the rind in fine strips, place in a saucepan and cover with cold water. Bring to the boil and simmer for 5 minutes. Drain.

3 Squeeze the juice from both fruits. Pour into a clean pan and add the redcurrant jelly. Stir until the jelly has dissolved. Simmer for 5 minutes, then add the port and stir to combine.

4 Blend the arrowroot and 10 ml (2 tsp) water to a smooth cream. Stir into the redcurrant mixture, off the heat.

5 Return to the heat and simmer, stirring, until the sauce thickens and clears. Add the strips of rind and serve immediately.

MINT SAUCE

Traditionally served with lamb

Makes about 300 ml (½ pint)

| 100 g (4 oz) fresh mint, finely chopped |
| 225 g (8 oz) granulated sugar |
| 300 ml (½ pint) vinegar |

1 Put the chopped mint into dry, wide-necked clean jars. Put the sugar and vinegar in a saucepan and heat gently until the sugar has dissolved, stirring with a wooden spoon.

2 Bring to the boil, then remove from the heat and leave until cold. Pour over the mint and cover the jars with airtight and vinegar-proof lids. Store in a cool, dry, dark place for up to 1 year.

3 To serve, lift out sufficient mint with a wooden spoon, together with a little of the liquid. Put into a jug or sauceboat and add a little fresh vinegar.

MINT JELLY

Serve with lamb, as an alternative to mint sauce

| 2.3 kg (5 lb) cooking apples |
| a few sprigs of fresh mint |
| 1.1 litres (2 pints) distilled vinegar |
| granulated sugar |
| 90–120 ml (6–8 tbsp) chopped fresh mint |
| a few drops of green food colouring |

1 Remove any bruised or damaged portions from the apples and roughly chop them into thick chunks without peeling or removing the cores.

2 Place the apples in a large saucepan with 1.1 litres (2 pints) water and the mint sprigs. Bring to the boil, then simmer gently for about 45 minutes until soft and pulpy. Stir from time to time to prevent sticking. Add the vinegar and boil for a further 5 minutes.

3 Spoon the apple pulp into a jelly bag or cloth attached to the legs of an upturned stool. Leave to strain into a large bowl for at least 12 hours.

4 Discard the pulp remaining in the jelly bag. Measure the extract and put it in a preserving pan with 450 g (1 lb) sugar for each 600 ml (1 pint) extract.

5 Heat gently, stirring, until the sugar has dissolved, then boil rapidly for about 10 minutes.

6 Test for a set: the jelly is ready when the temperature reaches 104°C (222°F) on a sugar thermometer, or when a spoonful of jelly on a chilled saucer wrinkles when you push your finger through. When setting point is reached, take the pan off the heat and remove any scum.

7 Stir in the chopped mint and add a few drops of green food colouring. Allow to cool slightly, then stir well to distribute the mint. Pour into warmed jars. Place a disc of waxed paper, waxed side down, across the surface of the jelly, then cover the jar with dampened Cellophane. Secure with an elastic band. Store up to 1 year in a cool, dry, dark place.

APPLE SAUCE

Serve with roast pork

Makes 300 ml ($\frac{1}{2}$ pint)

450 g (1 lb) cooking apples, peeled, cored and sliced

25 g (1 oz) butter or margarine

30–60 ml (2–4 tbsp) sugar

1 Put the apples in a saucepan with 30–45 ml (2–3 tbsp) water. Cook gently for about 10 minutes, until soft. Beat the fruit well, then purée in a blender or food processor, or press through a sieve with the back of a spoon.

2 Beat the butter into the mixture and sweeten to taste. Serve hot or cold.

SAUCE SOUBISE (ONION SAUCE)

Goes especially well with lamb

Serves 4–6

225 g (8 oz) onions, skinned and very finely chopped

25 g (1 oz) butter or margarine

a little stock or water

300 ml ($\frac{1}{2}$ pint) béchamel sauce (page 158)

salt and freshly ground pepper

1 Put the onions in a heavy-based saucepan. Add the butter and enough stock or water to moisten. Cook gently for about 15–20 minutes until soft.

2 Sieve or purée the onions in a blender or food processor. Mix the purée and béchamel sauce together in a clean saucepan. Add salt and pepper to taste and heat through for 1–2 minutes, stirring. Serve hot.

STUFFINGS

APPLE AND PRUNE STUFFING

Use with pork

Serves 4

225 g (8 oz) cooking apples, peeled and cored

100 g (4 oz) prunes, soaked and stoned

100 g (4 oz) cooked rice (about 40 g [1$\frac{1}{2}$ oz] raw weight)

50 g (2 oz) shredded suet

50 g (2 oz) almonds, blanched and chopped

finely grated rind and juice of $\frac{1}{2}$ lemon

salt and freshly ground pepper

1 egg, beaten

1 Chop the apples roughly. Cut the prunes into quarters. Place in a bowl with the remaining ingredients. Mix well together.

APRICOT STUFFING

Good with breast of lamb

Serves 4

50 g (2 oz) butter or margarine

1 medium onion, skinned and finely chopped

finely grated rind and juice of 1 small orange

175 g (6 oz) fresh breadcrumbs

100 g (4 oz) dried apricots, finely chopped

50 g (2 oz) salted peanuts, finely chopped

15 ml (1 tbsp) chopped fresh parsley

5 ml (1 tsp) curry powder

salt and freshly ground pepper

1 egg, size 6, beaten

1 Melt the butter in a small saucepan, add the onion and orange rind, cover and cook gently for 15 minutes until soft.

2 Meanwhile, put the breadcrumbs in a bowl with the apricots, peanuts and parsley. Stir well to mix.

3 Remove the onion with a slotted spoon and add to the stuffing mixture.

4 Sprinkle the curry powder into the residual butter and cook gently, stirring, for 1 minute. Pour in 45 ml (3 tbsp) orange juice and bring to the boil.

5 Mix the curried orange juice into the stuffing. Add salt and pepper to taste, then bind with the beaten egg.

RICE STUFFING

Use with lamb or pork

Serves 4

50 g (2 oz) long grain rice, cooked

1 chicken liver, trimmed and chopped

1 small onion, skinned and chopped

50 g (2 oz) raisins

50 g (2 oz) blanched almonds, chopped

30 ml (2 tbsp) chopped fresh parsley

25 g (1 oz) butter or margarine, melted

salt and freshly ground pepper

1 egg, beaten

1 Put all the ingredients in a bowl and mix well together using a wooden spoon.

SAGE AND ONION STUFFING

Use with pork

Serves 4

2 large onions, skinned and chopped

25 g (1 oz) butter or margarine

100 g (4 oz) fresh white breadcrumbs

10 ml (2 tsp) dried sage, or 30 ml (2 tbsp) chopped fresh sage

salt and freshly ground pepper

1 Put the onions into cold water, bring to the boil and cook for about 10 minutes, or until quite tender. Drain them well and mix with the other ingredients.

MUSHROOM AND HAM STUFFING

Use with lamb

Serves 4

25 g (1 oz) butter or margarine

100 g (4 oz) mushrooms, chopped

1 small onion, skinned and chopped

50 g (2 oz) streaky bacon, rinded and chopped

100 g (4 oz) cooked ham, chopped

15 ml (1 tbsp) chopped fresh parsley

salt and freshly ground pepper

1 Melt the butter in a saucepan, add the mushrooms and onion and fry gently for 10 minutes until soft but not coloured.

2 Add the bacon and cook over high heat for 2 minutes, stirring constantly. Stir in the chopped ham, parsley and salt and pepper to taste.

BRAZILIAN STUFFING

Use with pork

Serves 4

30 ml (2 tbsp) olive oil

1 small onion, skinned and chopped

1 garlic clove, skinned and finely chopped

½ green pepper, cored, seeded and chopped

2 tomatoes, skinned and chopped

25 g (1 oz) sultanas

4 olives, stoned and sliced

50 g (2 oz) brown rice, cooked

salt and freshly ground pepper

1 Heat the oil in a frying pan, add the onion and cook for 3–4 minutes, until soft. Add the remaining ingredients and cook for about 10 minutes until they pulp slightly together.

CELERY STUFFING

Use with pork and lamb

Serves 4

4 celery sticks, trimmed and finely sliced

1 onion, skinned and finely chopped

30 ml (2 tbsp) vegetable oil

grated rind and juice of 1 orange

salt and freshly ground pepper

100 g (4 oz) fresh white breadcrumbs

1 Put the celery in a saucepan, cover with boiling water and simmer for 15–20 minutes, until the celery is tender.

2 Heat the oil in a small pan, add the onion and fry for 5 minutes until golden brown.

3 Drain the celery and put it in a bowl; mix with the onion, orange rind and juice. Season well and add the breadcrumbs. Mix together thoroughly.

HERB STUFFING

Use with lamb

Serves 4

50 g (2 oz) bacon, rinded and chopped

45 ml (3 tbsp) shredded suet

100 g (4 oz) fresh white breadcrumbs

15 ml (1 tbsp) chopped fresh parsley

30 ml (2 tbsp) chopped fresh mixed herbs or 10 ml (2 tsp) dried mixed herbs

grated rind of ½ lemon

1 egg, beaten

salt and freshly ground pepper

1 Fry the bacon in its own fat without browning. Mix it with the suet, breadcrumbs, parsley, herbs, lemon rind, egg and seasoning.

MARINADES

WINE AND BAY MARINADE FOR LAMB

For every 450 g (1 lb) lamb use:

150 ml (¼ pint) red wine

45 ml (3 tbsp) wine vinegar

15 ml (1 tbsp) olive oil

6 bay leaves

1 Mix together the red wine and vinegar, then stir in the remaining ingredients. Season.

MARINADE FOR LAMB

For every 900 g (2 lb) lamb use:

75 ml (3 fl oz) red wine

60 ml (4 tbsp) olive oil

2.5 ml (½ tsp) dried thyme

2.5 ml (½ tsp) ground cumin

2.5 ml (½ tsp) dried marjoram

1 garlic clove, skinned and crushed

5 ml (1 tsp) lemon or lime juice

1 Mix together the red wine and olive oil, then stir in the remaining ingredients. Season.

MARINADE FOR PORK

For every 900 g (2 lb) pork use:

150 ml (¼ pint) dry white wine

45 ml (3 tbsp) vinegar

4 garlic cloves, skinned and crushed

1.25 ml (¼ tsp) ground cloves

1 Mix together the wine and the vinegar, then stir in the remaining ingredients. Season.

LEMON AND HERB MARINADE FOR PORK

For every 450 g (1 lb) pork use:

45 ml (3 tbsp) lemon juice

45 ml (3 tbsp) olive oil

3 parsley stalks, bruised

1.25 ml (¼ tsp) dried thyme

1 bay leaf

1 Mix together the lemon juice and oil, then stir in the remaining ingredients. Season.

Pâtés, Terrines and Sausages

Pâtés are simple to make and the ingredients used very flexible, so you can develop your own favourite combinations. If the mixture is cooked and served cold in its baking dish, it is called either a terrine (which is often more coarsely cut) or a pâté. If it is moulded in a pastry crust, it is a pâté en croûte.

INGREDIENTS

Ingredients for pâtés vary greatly, but they must contain a reasonable amount of fat, to make the pâté moist. For a meat pâté, pork fat is the best choice, or alternatively fat bacon. A mixture of lean pork and belly pork is often used and can be minced coarse or smooth depending on the texture you require. Liver, either lamb's or pig's, enriches the pâté, and flavourings can also be added. These include wine, brandy, port, herbs, spices and even truffles.

CHOPPING THE MEAT

A purist will say that the only satisfactory way to chop meat for a pâté is by hand. This can be a lengthy process, and the advent of food processors makes light work of it. Alternatively, pass cubes of meat through a mincer using fine or coarse blades according to the desired texture. For a very fine-textured pâté, you may have to pass the meat through the blades several times. When using a blender or food processor to prepare a pâté, mix the different meats before processing them. The meats can then be blended together in one operation. To give the pâté an interesting texture, strips or chunks of pork or ham

Strips of ham provide texture

can be embedded in the pâté before cooking. Alternatively, add 1 or more layers of attractive or brightly coloured ingredients such as pistachio nuts, green peppercorns, stuffed olives or pimientos.

BAKING DISHES

A pâté can be cooked in whatever ovenproof dish you have available, but bear in the mind that the cooking time will be determined by the depth of the pâté rather than the size of dish. Terrines made of cast iron, china and earthenware are available, but any shaped mould is suitable, such as a soufflé dish, cake or loaf tin.

STORING PÂTÉ

Home-made pâté will keep for up to 10 days in the refrigerator, or will freeze for up to 3 months.

HOW TO LINE A MOULD WITH STREAKY BACON RASHERS

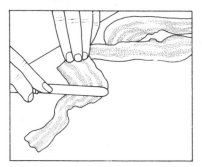

1 Remove the rind from the bacon with kitchen scissors. Stretch the rashers with the back of a heavy knife.

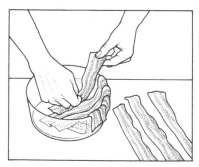

2 Line the mould with overlapping strips of bacon. Spoon the pâté into the mould, pressing down with the back of the spoon.

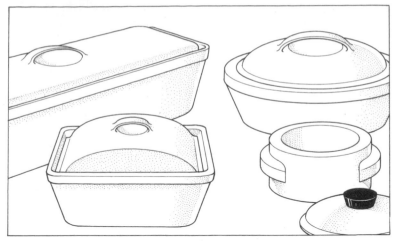

Pâtés can be made in dishes of many materials and shapes

3 Fold over any overhanging ends of bacon. Cover the top of the pâté with bacon strips.

HOW TO COOK IN A BAIN MARIE

1 Cover the top of the pâté with foil, sealing the edges well. Place the mould in a roasting tin or large pan.

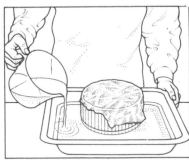

2 Pour enough boiling water into the tin to come halfway up the sides of the mould.

3 Place the tin in the oven to cook. Check the water level from time to time and add more boiling water as necessary.

4 Check the pâté is cooked by pressing it. When cooked, it will feel firm. Also the juices surrounding the pâté will be clear and the pâté will have shrunk from the sides of the mould.

HOW TO MAKE PÂTÉ EN CROÛTE

1 Roll out 2 pieces of puff pastry 5 cm (2 inches) larger all round than the size of the pâté.

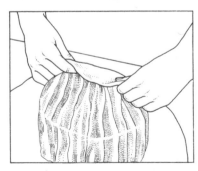

2 Place the pâté in the centre of one piece of pastry and brush the edges with beaten egg. Place remaining pastry on top, pressing edges together to seal.

3 Cut any trimmings of pastry into small decorative shapes. Brush pastry case with beaten egg and place the pastry shapes on top. Brush again with more egg.

4 Make a small hole in the centre of the pastry to allow steam to escape. Bake the pâté on a baking sheet in the oven at 200°C (400°F) mark 6 for about 25 minutes, depending on the size. Leave to cool, then chill.

HOW TO MAKE SAUSAGES

If you want to fill the sausage mixture into casings, a butcher who makes his own sausages may be prepared to sell a small quantity of skins. Natural sausage skins are also available by mail order from some companies. Filling skins by hand is messy; a wide-necked funnel can help and some food mixers have a sausage filling attachment. Basic sausage making kits are also available.

This basic recipe for pork sausages makes about 1.1 kg ($2\frac{1}{2}$ lb) or 20 good-sized sausages. Keep refrigerated and eat within 24 hours or freeze for up to 3 months. An electric mincer makes preparing the ingredients easier.

PORK SAUSAGES

225 g (8 oz) bread (2–3 days old)

700 g ($1\frac{1}{2}$ lb) lean pork

225 g (8 oz) firm pork fat (reduce the fat and increase the lean pork for a meatier sausage)

5 ml (1 tsp) salt

3.75 ml ($\frac{3}{4}$ tsp) ground mace

1.25 ml ($\frac{1}{4}$ tsp) ground ginger

good pinch of dried sage

freshly ground pepper

sausage casings or a little flour

1 Discard the crusts and cut the bread into cubes. Place in a bowl with 450 ml ($\frac{3}{4}$ pint) water.

2 Pass the meat and fat through the coarse plate of a mincer, then mix in remaining ingredients.

3 Squeeze out the excess water from the bread and mix into the meat mixture, making sure the bread is not lumpy. Pass through fine plate of mincer.

4 Either fill the mixture into skins, packing it well and giving a double twist every 8– 10 cm ($3\frac{1}{4}$–4 inches), or for skinless sausages form pieces of the mixture into sausage shapes on a floured board. Fry or grill for about 20 minutes.

Vegetable and Fruit Dishes

The finishing touch to any lamb or pork dish is its accompaniment, which can vary from a hot vegetable dish, that can often be cooked in the oven alongside the meat, to piquant pickled fruits which enhance cold meat meals.

RED CABBAGE BRAISED WITH APPLE

Serve with pork

Serves 4

25 g (1 oz) butter or margarine

1 medium onion, skinned and chopped

450 g (1 lb) red cabbage, trimmed and finely shredded

2 cooking apples, peeled, cored and sliced

150 ml ($\frac{1}{4}$ pint) red wine or chicken stock

15 ml (1 tbsp) soft brown sugar

15 ml (1 tbsp) wine vinegar

10 ml (2 tsp) lemon juice

pinch of ground cloves

salt and freshly ground pepper

1 Melt the butter in a large flameproof casserole, add the onion and cook gently for about 10 minutes until soft but not coloured.

2 Remove from the heat and add the remaining ingredients. Stir well to mix.

3 Cover tightly and cook in the oven at 170°C (325°F) mark 3 for 3–4 hours until tender. Serve piping hot.

RATATOUILLE

Serve with hot or cold lamb or pork

Serves 4

30 ml (2 tbsp) vegetable oil

25 g (1 oz) butter or margarine

4 tomatoes, skinned and sliced

2 aubergines, sliced

1 small green pepper, cored, seeded and sliced

2 onions, skinned and sliced

1 garlic clove, skinned and crushed

salt and freshly ground pepper

1 Heat the oil and butter in a flameproof casserole. Add the prepared vegetables, garlic and salt and pepper to taste.

2 Stir well, cover tightly and cook in the oven at 180°C (350°F) mark 4 for 1–1$\frac{1}{2}$ hours until the vegetables are tender. Serve hot or cold.

BRAISED LEEKS

A traditional accompaniment to pork

Serves 4

8 medium leeks, about 900 g (2 lb) total weight

125 g (4 oz) rindless streaky bacon

25 g (1 oz) butter or margarine

150 ml ($\frac{1}{4}$ pint) chicken stock

2 bay leaves

salt and freshly ground pepper

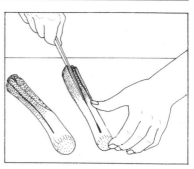

1 Trim off and discard the coarse, dark green leaves from the leeks. Split the leeks open without cutting in half and wash under cold running water to remove all grit.

2 Snip the bacon into small pieces. Melt the butter in a shallow flameproof casserole, add the leeks and bacon and fry gently until golden. Stir in the stock, add the bay leaves and salt and pepper to taste and bring to the boil.

3 Cover tightly and bake in the oven at 170°C (325°F) mark 3 for about 1 hour, or until the leeks are just tender but not mushy. Serve hot.

MUSHROOM-STUFFED TOMATOES

Traditional with lamb

Serves 4

4 large tomatoes
50 g (2 oz) button mushrooms
40 g (1½ oz) butter or margarine
1 small onion, skinned and finely chopped
1 celery stick, trimmed and finely chopped
30 ml (2 tbsp) fresh breadcrumbs
45 ml (3 tbsp) milk
10 ml (2 tsp) chopped fresh parsley
salt and freshly ground pepper
1 egg yolk, beaten

1 Cut the tops off the tomatoes, scoop out the flesh with a sharp-edged teaspoon and discard. Turn the tomato cases upside down and leave to drain.

2 Reserve 4 mushrooms caps and chop the remainder finely, with the stalks. Melt 25 g (1 oz) of the butter in a saucepan, add the chopped mushrooms, onion and celery and cook for 5 minutes.

3 Place the breadcrumbs in a small bowl. Add the milk and leave to stand for a few minutes.

4 Stir the breadcrumbs into the mushroom mixture with the parsley and salt and pepper to taste. Continue cooking until the mixture thickens. Remove from the heat and stir in the egg yolk.

5 Place the tomato cases in a greased ovenproof dish and fill with the stuffing. Melt the remaining butter in a clean pan and fry the mushroom caps for 5 minutes. Place a cap on each tomato. Cover and cook in the oven at 180°C (350°F) mark 4 for 10–15 minutes until the tomatoes are just tender. Serve hot.

SCALLOPED POTATOES

Serves 4

700 g (1½ lb) potatoes, peeled
45 ml (3 tbsp) plain flour
25 g (1 oz) butter or margarine
salt and freshly ground pepper
150 ml (¼ pint) milk or cream

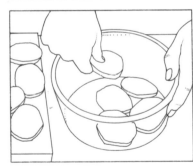

1 Slice the potatoes finely and arrange in layers in a greased ovenproof dish. In between each layer, dredge with flour, dot with butter and sprinkle with salt and freshly ground pepper.

2 Pour over the milk. Cook in the oven at 190°C (375°F) mark 5 for about 1¼ hours until the potato is tender when pierced with a skewer and the top is golden brown. Serve hot.

GOLDEN-BAKED CARROTS

Serves 4

6 large carrots, peeled
1 egg
45 ml (3 tbsp) plain flour
pinch of salt
75 g (3 oz) butter or margarine

1 Cut each carrot into quarters lengthways. Beat the egg lightly in a shallow dish. Stir the flour and salt together on a plate.

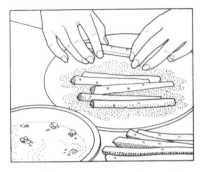

2 Dip each piece of carrot in the beaten egg and then coat in the flour.

3 Arrange in a greased ovenproof dish in one layer and dot with the butter.

4 Cover and cook in the oven at 190°C (375°F) mark 5 for 45 minutes.

5 Remove the lid and continue cooking for 15 minutes until the carrots are tender and golden brown. Serve hot.

ONIONS BAKED IN CIDER

Serves 4

450 g (1 lb) onions, skinned and thickly sliced
225 g (8 oz) cooking apples, peeled, cored and quartered
25 g (1 oz) butter or margarine
5 ml (1 tsp) sugar
salt and freshly ground pepper
150 ml ($\frac{1}{4}$ pint) cider

1 Place the onion and apple in a 1.1 litre (2 pint) casserole. Dot with the butter, then sprinkle over the sugar and salt and freshly ground pepper to taste.

2 Pour over the cider. Cover and cook in the oven at 180°C (350°F) mark 4 for 1$\frac{1}{2}$ hours.

3 Remove the lid and continue cooking for about 15 minutes until tender and golden brown. Serve hot.

SAUERKRAUT

A traditional, German accompaniment to bacon, pork and smoked sausages

15 g ($\frac{1}{2}$ oz) sea salt for each 450 g (1 lb) firm white cabbage

1 Trim the cabbage, discarding thick, woody stalks. Wash thoroughly, then shred finely.

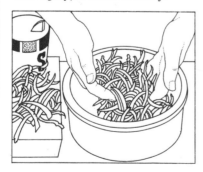

2 Put layers of shredded cabbage in a large stoneware jar (or crock) or wooden tub and sprinkle each layer with salt. Toss the cabbage with your hands, then pack down after each layer.

3 When the container is filled, cover the cabbage with a large piece of cling film (not foil). Put an inverted plate or lid on top and press down with a heavy, non-metal weight, such as a jar filled with water. Make sure it is airtight.

4 In a few days, the lid should be under the surface of the brine. Leave at room temperature for about 3 weeks, for fermentation to take place, removing any scum every few days, as necessary. If the level of brine falls, top it up with a solution of 25 g (1 oz) salt in 1.1 litres (2 pints) water.

5 After about 3 weeks, when the salted cabbage has stopped frothing and fermentation is complete, the cabbage is ready to use.

6 For storage, the sauerkraut must be bottled. Drain the brine into a large saucepan and bring to the boil. Add the cabbage and bring back to the boil, stirring occasionally. If liked, add caraway seeds or juniper berries.

7 Transfer at once into hot, clean jars, packing the sauerkraut down to remove any air pockets. Leave a headspace of about 2.5 cm (1 inch) at the top of the jars.

8 Put on rubber rings and glass caps or metal discs, but not screwbands or clips. Place the jars 5 cm (2 inches) apart on a solid baking sheet lined with newspaper. Put in the oven at 150°C (300°F) mark 2 for 25 minutes.

9 Remove the jars one by one, placing them on a wooden surface (anything colder than wood could cause the glass to crack). Put on clips or screw-bands, screwing the bands as tightly as possible. Allow to become quite cold before testing for a good seal.

10 Sauerkraut is generally heated for 10 minutes in its own liquid before serving.

FRUIT ACCOMPANIMENTS

SPICED PICKLED PEACHES

Serve with cold ham or cold roast pork

about 30 whole cloves
900 g (2 lb) peaches, skinned, stoned and halved
450 g (1 lb) granulated sugar
300 ml ($\frac{1}{2}$ pint) white wine vinegar
thinly pared rind of $\frac{1}{2}$ lemon
1 small cinnamon stick

1 Push 2 cloves into each peach half. Place the sugar, vinegar, lemon rind and cinnamon stick in a saucepan and heat gently, stirring, for about 5 minutes until the sugar has dissolved.

2 Add the peach halves to the pan and simmer the fruit in the sweetened vinegar for about 5 minutes until soft.

3 Remove the fruit with a slotted spoon and pack into warmed, clean jars. Continue boiling the vinegar until slightly reduced and beginning to thicken.

4 Strain the vinegar syrup and pour sufficient over the fruit to cover. Cover the jars immediately with airtight and vinegar-proof tops. Store in a cool, dry dark place for 2–3 months before use.

PICKLED ORANGE RINGS

Serve as an accompaniment to cold ham

6 firm oranges, wiped
900 ml (1½ pints) distilled vinegar
700 g (1½ lb) granulated sugar
20 ml (4 tsp) ground cloves
7.5 cm (3 inch) cinnamon stick
5 ml (1 tsp) whole cloves

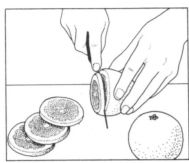

1 Slice the oranges into rounds 0.5 cm (¼ inch) thick. Put the fruit into a large saucepan with just enough water to cover and simmer gently for 45 minutes until the rind is very soft.

2 Remove the oranges with a slotted spoon and add the vinegar, sugar, ground cloves and cinnamon to the juice in the pan. Bring to the boil and simmer gently for 10 minutes.

3 Return the orange rings to the pan, a few at a time, and cook gently until the rind becomes transparent.

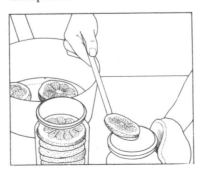

4 Using a slotted spoon, lift the orange rings from the syrup and pack into warmed, clean jars.

5 Continue to boil the syrup for about 15 minutes until it begins to thicken. Leave to cool slightly, then pour it over the orange rings. Add a few whole cloves to each jar and cover immediately with airtight and vinegar-proof tops. Store in a cool, dry, dark place for 2–3 months before use.

SPICED PEARS

Delicious with cold pork

900 g (2 lb) firm eating pears, peeled, cored and quartered
450 ml (¾ pint) cider vinegar
450 g (1 lb) granulated sugar
1 cinnamon stick
10 whole cloves
1 small piece of fresh root ginger, peeled

1 Place the pears in a saucepan and cover with boiling water. Cook gently for about 5 minutes until almost tender, then drain.

2 Pour the vinegar into a clean pan. Add 300 ml (½ pint) cold water, the sugar, cinnamon, cloves and root ginger. Heat gently, stirring, until the sugar has dissolved, then boil for 5 minutes.

3 Add the pears and continue cooking until the pears are transparent. Remove the pears with a slotted spoon and pack them into warmed, clean jars.

4 Strain the vinegar syrup to remove the spices and pour over the pears to cover. Cover the jars with airtight and vinegar-proof tops. Store in a cool, dry, dark place for 2–3 months before use.

Basic Recipes

There are pancakes, tortillas and pastries here for wrapping up or covering meat dishes. Also included are two clever ideas for using up leftover roast lamb. Reheating leftover pork is not a good idea, for health reasons.

PANCAKES

Makes 8 pancakes

125 g (4 oz) plain flour

pinch of salt

1 egg

300 ml (½ pint) milk

vegetable oil, for frying

1 Mix the flour and salt together in a bowl. Make a well in the centre and break in the egg. Add the half the milk. Gradually work in the flour. Beat until smooth.

2 Add the remaining milk gradually. Beat until the ingredients are well mixed.

3 Heat a little oil in an 18 cm (7 inch) heavy-based pancake or frying pan running it around to coat the sides of the pan. Pour off any surplus.

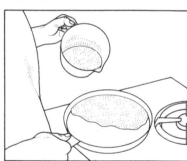

4 Raise the handle side of the pan slightly. Pour a little batter in from the raised side.

5 Place over moderate heat and cook until the pancake begins to brown underneath. Turn with a palette knife and cook the other side until golden brown. Slide the pancake on to a warmed plate lined with greaseproof paper.

6 Continue cooking the batter to make 8 pancakes, adding a little oil to the pan each time. Stack the pancakes up on the plate, interleaving each one with greaseproof paper.

MEXICAN TORTILLAS

For a mouthwatering recipe using these tortillas, try Burritos (page 26) with a meat and red kidney bean filling.

Makes about 10

250 g (9 oz) plain flour (see below)

40 g (1½ oz) lard

5 ml (1 tsp) salt

225 ml (8 fl oz) tepid water

1 Mix the plain flour with the salt in a large bowl. Rub in the fat as for shortcrust pastry. Gradually add the tepid water, mixing lightly with a fork to make a dough that is just moist enough to hold together. If necessary add more water, about 15 ml (1 tbsp) at a time. Gather the dough up lightly into a ball.

2 Knead the dough quickly and lightly in the bowl with one hand until it is smooth and free from cracks.

3 Divide the dough into 10 equal pieces and shape each one into a small ball. Keep the dough balls covered to prevent them drying while you roll out each one.

4 Flatten each ball until 0.5 cm (¼ inch) thick, then place between 2 sheets of waxed paper. Roll out to 20.5 cm (8 inch) rounds, 0.25 cm ($\frac{1}{16}$ inch) thick and leave the tortillas between the waxed paper.

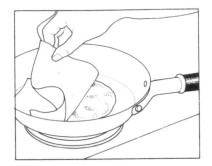

5 Remove the top sheet from one round and invert it on to a hot, ungreased frying pan. Peel off the second sheet of paper. Cook for 40 seconds or until small bubbles appear.

6 Turn the tortilla over and cook for a further 30 seconds or until the underside is speckled with brown.

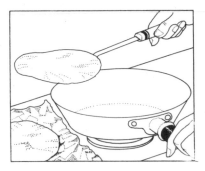

7 Remove from the frying pan. Place the tortilla on a sheet of foil and wrap it to keep hot while you cook the remainder, stacking them in the foil as they are cooked.

Note: tortillas are usually made with cornmeal flour, called masa harina, and are only about 15 cm (6 inches) in diameter. Masa harina is not readily available, but if you are able to obtain it then you can use it to make tortillas as here, in the proportion of 350 g (12 oz) masa harina to 300 ml ($\frac{1}{2}$ pint) hot water, omitting the fat. A tortilla press, available from good kitchen shops, is essential for making cornmeal tortillas.

SHORTCRUST PASTRY

For any quantity of shortcrust pastry, always use half fat to flour

225 g (8 oz) plain flour
pinch of salt
50 g (2 oz) butter or block margarine
50 g (2 oz) lard

1 Sift the flour and salt together in a bowl. Cut the butter and lard into small pieces and add to the flour.

2 Lightly rub the butter and lard into the flour with your fingertips until the mixture resembles fine breadcrumbs.

3 Add 30–45 ml (2–3 tbsp) chilled water evenly over the surface. Stir in with a round-bladed knife until the mixture begins to stick together in lumps.

4 With one hand, collect the mixture together to form a ball. Knead lightly for a few seconds to give a firm, smooth dough. Do not over-handle.

5 The pastry can be used straight away, but it is better if allowed to 'rest' for about 30 minutes wrapped in foil in the refrigerator.

6 Roll out the pastry on a lightly floured surface to a thickness about 0.25 cm ($\frac{1}{8}$ inch). Do not pull or stretch the pastry. To cook, the usual oven temperature is 200–220°C (400–425°F) mark 6–7.

HOT-WATER CRUST PASTRY

450 g (1 lb) plain flour
10 ml (2 tsp) salt
100 g (4 oz) lard, or lard and butter

1 Mix the flour and salt together in a bowl. Make a well in the centre. In a small saucepan, melt the lard in 250 ml (9 fl oz) water, then bring to the boil and pour into the well.

2 Working quickly, beat with a wooden spoon to form a fairly soft dough.

3 Using one hand, pinch the dough lightly together and knead until smooth and silky.

4 Cover with cling film or a damp tea towel. Leave in a warm place to rest for 20–30 minutes for the dough to become elastic and easy to work. Use as required, but do not allow to cool and harden. The usual oven temperature is 220°C (425°F) mark 7, reducing to 180°C (350°F) mark 4.

WHITE SAUCE

Makes 300 ml ($\frac{1}{2}$ pint) pouring sauce

15 g ($\frac{1}{2}$ oz) butter or margarine
15 g ($\frac{1}{2}$ oz) plain flour
300 ml ($\frac{1}{2}$ pint) milk
salt and freshly ground pepper

1 Melt the butter in a saucepan, add the flour and cook gently, stirring, for 1–2 minutes. Do not allow the mixture to brown.

2 Remove from the heat and gradually blend in the milk, stirring after each addition to prevent lumps forming.

3 Bring to the boil slowly, stirring constantly, then simmer for 3 minutes until thickened and smooth. Add salt and pepper to taste.

──── VARIATIONS ────

Coating sauce: follow the White Sauce recipe above, but increase both the butter and flour to 25 g (1 oz) each.

Cheese sauce: follow the recipe for White Sauce or Coating sauce above. Before seasoning with salt and pepper, stir in 50 g (2 oz) finely grated Cheddar cheese, 2.5–5 ml ($\frac{1}{2}$–1 tsp) prepared mustard and a pinch of cayenne.

BÉCHAMEL SAUCE

Makes about 300 ml (½ pint)

300 ml (½ pint) milk

1 small onion, skinned and quartered

1 small carrot, peeled and sliced

½ small celery stick, trimmed and sliced

2 cloves

6 white peppercorns

1 blade of mace

sprig of parsley

sprig of thyme

1 bay leaf

25 g (1 oz) butter or margarine

25 g (1 oz) plain flour

salt and freshly ground pepper

1 Put the milk into a saucepan with the onion, carrot, celery, the spices and the herbs. Slowly bring just to the boil, then remove from the heat and cover the pan. Infuse for 30 minutes. Strain, reserving the milk.

2 Melt the butter in a saucepan, add the flour and cook gently, stirring, for 1–2 minutes. Do not allow the mixture to brown.

3 Remove from the heat and gradually blend in the flavoured milk.

4 Bring to the boil slowly, stirring constantly, then simmer for 3 minutes until thick. Add salt and pepper

SIMPLE TOMATO SAUCE

Serves 4

450 g (1 lb) tomatoes, skinned and roughly chopped, or 397 g (14 oz) can tomatoes, with their juice

1 small onion, skinned and roughly chopped

1 garlic clove, skinned and chopped

1 celery stick, trimmed and sliced

1 bay leaf

sprig of parsley

2.5 ml (½ tsp) sugar

salt and freshly ground pepper

1 Place all the ingredients in a saucepan and bring to the boil. Simmer, uncovered, for 30 minutes until thickened. Stir occasionally to prevent sticking.

2 Remove the bay leaf and purée the mixture in a blender or food processor until smooth, or push through a sieve using a wooden spoon. Reheat and then taste and adjust seasoning.

USING LEFTOVER LAMB

LAMB CRUMBLE

Serves 4

350 g (12 oz) cooked roast lamb

1 medium onion, skinned

115 g (4½ oz) plain flour

15 ml (1 tbsp) tomato purée

300 ml (½ pint) lamb or beef stock

salt and freshly ground pepper

50 g (2 oz) butter or margarine

50 g (2 oz) Cheddar cheese, grated

2.5 ml (½ tsp) dried mixed herbs

1 Mince together the meat and onion. Place in a bowl and mix in 15 g (½ oz) of the flour, the tomato purée, stock and salt and pepper to taste. Turn into a shallow ovenproof dish.

2 Put the remaining flour in a clean bowl. Rub in the butter until the mixture resembles fine breadcrumbs, then stir in the grated cheese, herbs and salt and pepper to taste. Spoon the crumble over the meat.

3 Bake in the oven at 190°C (375°F) mark 5 for 45 minutes to 1 hour until golden brown.

PILAFF

Serves 4–6

350 g (12 oz) Basmati rice

75 g (3 oz) butter or margarine

1 onion, skinned and chopped

2 large garlic cloves, skinned and finely chopped

2.5 ml (½ tsp) ground cumin

2.5 ml (½ tsp) ground coriander

8 cardamom pods, crushed

1.1 litres (2 pints) hot lamb stock

salt and freshly ground pepper

15 ml (1 tbsp) olive oil

50 g (2 oz) flaked almonds

225 g (8 oz) cooked lamb, diced

50 g (2 oz) seedless raisins

fresh coriander, to garnish

1 Rinse the rice under cold running water. Drain well. Melt 50 g (2 oz) of the butter in a large flameproof casserole, add the onion and garlic and fry gently until soft and golden.

2 Add the rice, cumin and ground coriander and fry, stirring, until the grains of rice begin to look transparent. Add the cardamoms, then pour in the hot stock and bring to the boil. Add salt and pepper to taste and stir once. Lower the heat, cover and simmer gently for 15 minutes.

3 Meanwhile, heat 15 g (½ oz) of the butter and the oil in a separate pan. Add the almonds and fry until golden brown, shaking the pan constantly. Drain on absorbent kitchen paper.

4 Add the lamb to the rice, cover again and simmer for 10 minutes until the rice is tender.

5 Fork two-thirds of the almonds into the rice with the raisins and the remaining butter. Cover, turn off the heat and leave to stand for 5 minutes. Serve hot, garnished with remaining almonds and coriander.

INDEX

Apple:
　Apple and prune stuffing 148
　Apple sauce 148
　Cider pork sauté 121
　Huntingdon fidget pie 96
　Normandy pork 118
　Red cabbage braised with
　　apple 152
　Sausage and apple plait 37
Apricot:
　Apricot stuffing 148
　Colonial goose 87
　Persian lamb and apricot
　　stew 122

Bacon. *See also* Gammon
　To bake, boil, braise, fry or
　　grill bacon 141
　To buy bacon 140
　To freeze bacon 142, 143
　To prepare bacon for cooking
　　140
　To store bacon 140
　Bacon in cider with sage and
　　onion dumplings 18
　Bacon and mushroom
　　pancakes 24
　Cheese and bacon quiche 43
　Cuts of bacon 140
　Glazes for baked bacon 146
　Huntingdon fidget pie 96
　Lentil, bacon and vegetable
　　soup 90
　Liver and bacon with
　　potato pancakes 111
　Peanut glazed bacon hock 16
Barbecued spareribs 93
Bean:
　Chilli pork and beans 94
　Chipolatas and beans 60
Béchamel sauce 158
Bigos 78
Boiling 135
Boning knives 135
Boning lamb or pork 136–7
Braising 134
Brazilian stuffing 149
Burritos 26
Butcher's knives 135
Butters, savoury 146

Cabbage. *See also* Red cabbage
　Polish cabbage and meat 78
　Sauerkraut 154
　Stuffed cabbage rolls 27
Carrot:
　Golden-baked carrots 153
Carving 138–9
Casseroling 134
Caucasian lamb kebabs 81
Celery stuffing 149
Cheese:
　Cheese and bacon quiche 43
　Cheese sauce 157
　Cheesy sausage rolls 34
　Ham and cheese rollups 55
　Ricotta cheese and ham pie
　　40
Chicken stock 144
Chilli pork and beans 94

Chinese pork broth 89
Chinese red-cooked pork 82
Chipolatas and beans 60
Choppers 135
Cider:
　Bacon in cider with sage and
　　onion dumplings 18
　Cider pork sauté 121
　Normandy pork 118
　Onions baked in cider 154
Coating sauce 157
Colonial goose 87
Crown roast of lamb 9
Cucumber, minted lamb
　burgers with 51
Cumberland sauce 147
Curry:
　Indian lamb and spinach
　　curry 84
Cypriot sausage kebabs 64

Daube d'agneau 75
Dolmas 33
Dumplings:
　Sage and onion dumplings
　　18

Equipment 135–6

Filet de porc chasseur 117
Freezing meat 142–3
French roast racks of lamb
　with rosemary and garlic 10
Fruit accompaniments 155
Fruity stuffed pork chops 99
Frying 134

Gammon 140:
　Party gammon 48
Garlic butter 146
Glazes for baked ham or bacon
　146
Golden-baked carrots 153
Gravy 145
Green butter 146
Grilling 134–5
Guard of honour, to make 137

Ham 140:
　To freeze ham 142, 143
　Glazes for baked ham 146
　Ham and cheese rollups 55
　Parma croissants 23
　Ricotta cheese and ham pie
　　40
Heart:
　Baked stuffed lamb's hearts
　　21
　Lamb's hearts 130
　Pig's hearts 132
Herb butter 146
Herb stuffing 149
Honey glaze, sharp 146
Hot-water crust pastry 157
Huntingdon fidget pie 96

Indian spiced lamb 84
Indian lamb and spinach curry
　84
Irish stew 67

Kebabs:
　Cypriot sausage kebabs 64

Lamb and pepper kebabs 52
　Shashlik 81
Kibbeh 77
Kidney:
　Lamb's kidneys 130
　Pig's kidneys 132
　Sautéed kidneys with
　　tomatoes 112
　Kidney-stuffed pork loin 15

Lamb. *See also* Heart, Kidney,
　Liver, Sweetbreads, Tongue
　To boil lamb 135
　To bone a leg, shoulder or
　　breast of lamb 136
　To braise lamb 134
　To carve lamb 138–9
　To casserole or stew lamb
　　134
　To choose and buy lamb 131
　To freeze lamb 142, 143
　To fry lamb 134
　To grill lamb 134–5
　To make a guard of honour
　　137
　To make noisettes of lamb 137
　To roast lamb 133–4
　To store lamb 131
　Colonial goose 87
　Crown roast of lamb 9
　Cuts of lamb 130
　Daube d'agneau 75
　Dolmas 33
　French roast racks of lamb
　　with rosemary and garlic 10
　Indian spiced lamb 84
　Indian lamb and spinach curry
　　84
　Irish stew 67
　Kibbeh 77
　Lamb chops ratatouille 126
　Lamb crumble 158
　Lamb cutlets Reform 71
　Lamb noisettes with
　　mushrooms and onions 116
　Lamb offal 130
　Lamb and pepper kebabs 52
　Lamb samosas 32
　Lamb and spinach lasagne 103
　Lamb stock 144
　Lamb in tomato sauce with
　　herb bread 100
　Lancashire hot pot 68
　Leftover lamb, recipes for 158
　Marinades for lamb 149
　Marinated lamb with onion
　　purée 107
　Minted lamb burgers with
　　cucumber 51
　Moussaka 63
　Mustard-coated leg of lamb 11
　Persian lamb and apricot stew
　　122
　Pilaff 158
　Rolled stuffed breasts of
　　lamb 12
　Sauces to serve with lamb
　　147–8
　Shashlik 81
　Sheftalia 64
　Shepherd's pie 113
　Spiced lentil bake 104
Lancashire hot pot 68

Larding needles 135
Lasagne:
　Lamb and spinach lasagne
　　103
Leek:
　Braised leeks 152
Lemon juice and herb marinade
　for pork 149
Lentil:
　Lentil, bacon and vegetable
　　soup 90
　Spiced lentil bake 104
Liver:
　Coarse liver pâté 44
　Lamb's liver 130
　Liver and bacon with potato
　　pancakes 111
　Liver goujons with orange
　　sauce 108
　Liver stroganoff 61
　Pig's liver 132

Maître d'hôtel butter 146
Marinades 149
Marinated lamb with onion
　purée 107
Marmalade and honey glaze,
　spiced 146
Meat glaze 145
Meat loaf 46
Mexican tortillas 156–7
Mint jelly 147
Mint sauce 147
Minted lamb burgers with
　cucumber 51
Mishmishiya 122
Moussaka 63
Mushroom:
　Bacon and mushroom
　　pancakes 24
　Lamb noisettes with
　　mushrooms and onions
　　116
　Mushroom and ham stuffing
　　149
　Mushroom-stuffed tomatoes
　　153
　Sweetbreads with mushrooms
　　and white wine 128
Mustard-coated leg of lamb 11

Noisettes of lamb, to make 137
Noisettes de porc touraine 125
Normandy pork 118

Onion:
　Lamb noisettes with
　　mushrooms and onions
　　116
　Marinated lamb with onion
　　purée 107
　Onion butter 146
　Onion sauce 148
　Onions baked in cider 154
Orange:
　Liver goujons with orange
　　sauce 108
　Orange and parsley butter
　　146
　Pickled orange rings 155

Pancakes:
　To make pancakes 156

Pancakes: (continued)
  Bacon and mushroom
    pancakes 24
  Mexican tortillas 156–7
  Potato pancakes 111
Parma croissants 23
Parsley butter 146
Party gammon 48
Pastry 157
Pâtés:
  To chop the meat 150
  To cook pâtés in a bain marie
    151
  To line a mould with streaky
    bacon 150
  To make pâté en croûte 151
  To store pâté 150
  Coarse liver pâté 44
Peach:
  Spiced pickled peaches 154
Peanut glazed bacon hock 16
Pear:
  Spiced pears 155
Persian lamb and apricot stew
  122
Pickled orange rings 155
Pies:
  Huntingdon fidget pie 96
  Pork and olive pie 41
  Raised pork pie 38
  Ricotta cheese and ham pie
    40
  Shepherd's pie 113
Pig's hearts, kidneys, liver
  132
Pilaff 158
Polish cabbage and meat 78
Pork. *See also* Sausages
  To boil pork 135
  To bone a leg of pork 136
  To bone a loin of pork 137
  To braise pork 134
  To carve pork 139
  To casserole or stew pork
    134
  To freeze pork 142, 143
  To fry pork 134
  To grill pork 134–5
  To roast pork 133–4
  To salt pork 132–3
  To store pork 132

Barbecued spareribs 93
Bigos 78
Burritos 26
Chilli pork and beans 94
Chinese pork broth 89
Chinese red-cooked pork 82
Cider pork sauté 121
Cuts of pork 131–2
Filet de porc chasseur 117
Fruity stuffed pork chops 99
Kidney-stuffed pork loin 15
Loin of pork with fruit
  stuffing 115
Marinades for pork 149
Meat loaf 46
Noisettes de porc touraine
  125
Normandy pork 118
Pork chops en croûte 31
Pork offal 132
Pork and olive pie 41
Pork paprikash 95
Pot roast of pork and red
  cabbage 17
Raised pork pie 38
Sauces to serve with pork
  148
Spanish pork escalopes 56
Spring rolls 29
Stir-fried pork and vegetables
  59
Stuffed cabbage rolls 27
Sweet and sour pork 82
Pot roast of pork and red
  cabbage 17
Potato:
  Potato pancakes 111
  Scalloped potatoes 153
Prune:
  Apple and prune stuffing
    148
  Noisettes de porc touraine
    125
Quiche:
  Cheese and bacon quiche 43

Raan 84
Raised pork pie 38
Ratatouille 152
Red cabbage braised with apple
  152

Red cabbage, pot roast of pork
  and 17
Reform sauce 71
Rice:
  Pilaff 158
  Rice stuffing 148
Ricotta cheese and ham pie 40
Roasting 133–4
Rolled stuffed breast of lamb
  12
Rosemary and garlic, French
  roast racks of lamb with 10

Sag gosht 84
Sage and onion dumplings 18
Sage and onion stuffing 148
Salt pork 132–3
Samosas 32
Sauces:
  Apple sauce 148
  Béchamel sauce 158
  Cheese sauce 157
  Coating sauce 157
  Cumberland sauce 147
  Mint jelly 147
  Mint sauce 147
  Reform sauce 71
  Sauce soubise (onion sauce)
    148
  White sauce 157
Sauerkraut 154
Sausage, sausagemeat:
  To make pork sausages 151
  Cheesy sausage rolls 34
  Chipolatas and beans 60
  Sausage and apple plait 37
  Spicy Scotch eggs 47
  Toad in the hole 72
Sautéed kidneys with tomatoes
  112
Savoury butters 146
Saws 135
Scalloped potatoes 153
Scotch eggs, spicy 47
Shashlik 81
Sheftalia 64
Shepherd's pie 113
Shortcrust pastry 157
Skewers 135
Soup:
  Chinese pork broth 89

Lentil, bacon and
  vegetable soup 90
Spanish pork escalopes 56
Spiced lentil bake 104
Spiced marmalade and honey
  glaze 146
Spiced pears 155
Spiced pickled peaches 154
Spicy Scotch eggs 47
Spinach:
  Indian lamb and spinach
    curry 84
  Lamb and spinach lasagne
    103
Spit roasting 134
Spring rolls 29
Stewing 134
Stir-fried pork and vegetables
  59
Stocks 144–5
Stuffed cabbage rolls 27
Stuffed vine leaves 33
Stuffings 148–9
Sweet and sour pork 82
Sweetbreads 131:
  Sweetbreads with mushrooms
    and white wine 128

Thawing meat 143
Toad in the hole 72
Tomato:
  Lamb in tomato sauce with
    herb bread 100
  Mushroom-stuffed tomatoes
    153
  Sautéed kidneys with
    tomatoes 112
Tongue:
  Lamb's tongues 130
Tortillas 156–7
Trussing needles 135

Vegetable accompaniments
  152–4
Vine leaves, stuffed 33

White sauce 157
White stock 145
Wine and bay marinade 149